YEADON'S REGISTER

of

L N E R

LOCOMOTIVES

Volume 3

RAVEN, THOMPSON & PEPPERCORN PACIFICS

Compiled by

W.B.YEADON

Copyright Booklaw/Railbus 2001
ISBN 1 871608 20 1

THE REGISTRAR

Of the 80 Pacifics detailed in this Volume, only five were in existence when the Registrar began his comprehensive study, and recording, of LNER locomotives. Recollection of the Raven Pacifics is still soured by the missed opportunity of acquiring a *CITY OF DURHAM* nameplate when he shared 2403's solitude in Darlington scrap yard. The first Thompson A2/1, No. 3696 was only 17 days old when he was hauled by it on the 2.11 p.m. ex–Darlington stopping train to Leeds. The A2/2 rebuild came his way in August 1946 when No. 502 *EARL MARISCHAL* took him in the 8.32 a.m. from Thornton Junction to Aberdeen. That was only three months too late to get its photo as a Pacific whilst still numbered 2002, the only one of the six still missing from his collection in their original numbers; can you fill that gap? The scratch built A2/3 was first sampled as early as 19th April 1947 when No. 511 *AIRBORNE* took him to Darlington on the 1.50 p.m. from Leeds. Thompson's desecration of 4470 *GREAT NORTHERN* was witnessed in Doncaster Works two weeks before the engine was released into traffic, through a friendship with Peter Townend, whilst he was still a Premium Apprentice there. First sight of 4470 in traffic, nine months later, brought forth a chuckle, for it was standing in Newark station on nothing better than the 7.42 a.m. *Parliamentary* all stations Doncaster to Grantham, whilst the Registrar hared past in the 7.30 a.m. Leeds to King's Cross, with Gresley Pacific *SOLARIO* in charge.

ACKNOWLEDGEMENTS

First, undoubtedly, to my wife for her continued patience at still having to cope with railway enthusiasm, often when her home is invaded by visitors, frequently at short notice. Then to those who, in amply sufficient numbers, have bought Volumes 1 and 2, which have made it viable for Irwell Press to continue the series. I still realise how much I am in debt to photographers who got themselves into the right place at the right time, alas an increasing number to whom I cannot now express my thanks personally. That also applies to many ex-railway employees who were sufficiently far-sighted to help me put on permanent record the result of their daily work, however humdrum it appeared to them at the time. Then my very sincere gratitude to Irwell Press in presenting it properly, and so attractively.

The Yeadon Collection is available for inspection and anyone who wishes to
inspect it should contact:-
The Archivist
Brynmor Jones Library
University of Hull
Hull
HU6 7RX
Tel: 01482-465265
A catalogue of the Yeadon collection is available.

First published in the United Kingdom by Irwell Press
Reprinted by BOOKLAW/RAILBUS 2001 in association with CHALLENGER
382 Carlton Hill, Nottingham NG4 1JA
www.booklawpublications.co.uk
www.booklawpublications.co.com

Printed and bound by The Amadeus Press, Cleckheaton.

CONTENTS

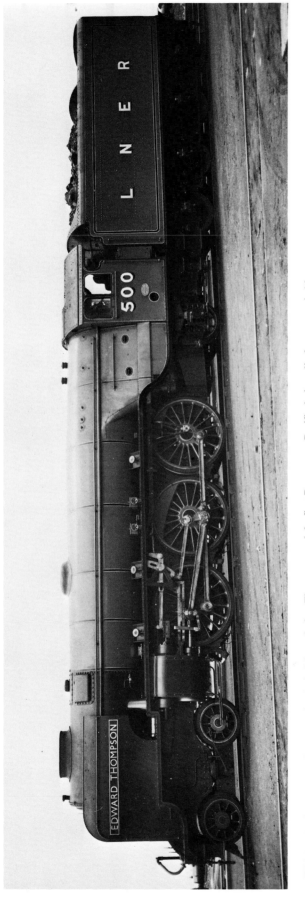

With barely eighteen months separating their debuts the last Thompson and the first Peppercorn Pacific designs display a remarkable contrast.

INTRODUCTION

Volumes 1 and 2 dealt with the work of one man – Gresley; this third volume describes how three other engineers provided the means for the same work. Raven and Thompson designs were no more than mediocre, which my dictionary defines as neither good nor bad. The two for which Peppercorn was responsible did prove worthy counterparts of the Gresley Pacifics.

In a work devoted to LNER Locomotives, some explanation is required for the inclusion of the Peppercorn A1 Class, for the first one was not completed until August 1948 and consequently never wore *any* LNER livery. Despite 16 being put on order from Doncaster Works on 9th November 1945 and another 23 from Darlington Works on 21st November 1947, their design owed nothing to Thompson, even if he was Chief Mechanical Engineer until 30th June 1946, when he retired. Whilst he was still in charge, Doncaster Drawing Office 'made haste with less speed' on scheming out these Pacifics during his last six months in office, and obviously the Traffic Department were not in urgent need of the extra power that they would provide. But three months before the end of the LNER, work on the final drawings was in full spate, so A1 Class can rightly be regarded as pure LNER.

The Raven Pacifics totalled no more than five – two built by the North Eastern Railway in 1922 and three by the LNER in 1924. The latter were authorised by the Locomotive Committee on 22nd February 1923 and at the same meeting it was rec-ommended that Gresley be appointed CME, which the Board approved at their meeting on the following day. The Raven Pacific was never more than a political answer to the first Gresley, Great Northern, Pacific of April 1922, being simply a stretched version of Raven's successful Atlantic, Class Z. At the end of June 1923 the first one was given a chance to be compared with the Gresley design, on trials between Kings Cross and Doncaster. It could show no advantage, so further building was limited to the three which were already under construction at Darlington.

Thompson succeeded Gresley on the latter's death in April 1941, knowing that he had only five years to retirement age and with the country mainly concerned with survival in a World War. Much of his work was, unfortunately, clouded, by what had every sign of a personal vendetta against Gresley design features. He introduced four Pacific classes, of which three were simply re-builds. The class he did start from scratch to become A2 Part 3, amply bore out the well established engineering maxim that 'if it doesn't look right, then it isn't right'. His three rebuilds never even equalled those from which they were derived and I can only present Thompson in a better light when a further Volume deals with his B1 Class 4-6-0. On Pacifics he is best quietly forgotten. Fortunately he went in time for Peppercorn to retrieve locomotive prestige for the LNER and for the Doncaster design team.

WORKS CODES

Cow – Cowlairs.
Dar – Darlington.
Don – Doncaster.
Gat – Gateshead.
Hay – Haymarket Shed.
Inv – Inverurie.

REPAIR CODES

C/H – Casual Heavy.
C/L – Casual Light.
G – General.
H – Heavy.
H/I – Heavy Intermediate.
L – Light.
L/I – Light Intermediate.
N/C – Non–Classified.

2400 in September 1923, north of Berwick with the up *Flying Scotsman.* Now in LNER painting, with cut–away lower corners to buffer beams but before the nameplates were fitted.

2401 coming south from Edinburgh in 1925, on an express for Kings Cross. In LNER livery and named, twin handles have replaced, in a minor change, the wheel and handle smokebox door fastening. Not until 1932 did Darlington put *CLASS A2* on the buffer beam, and until then, simply 4.6.2. had been displayed.

RAVEN A2

2400
CITY OF NEWCASTLE.

Darlington.

To traffic 12/1922.

REPAIRS:
Gat.18–19/6/23.**L.**
Don.5–14/7/23. *Painting to LNER livery.*
Dar.16/7–14/8/23.**L.**
Dar.4–8/9/23.**L.**
Dar.10–22/12/23.**L.** *Exhaust injector.*
Dar.19/1–28/4/25.**G.** *New crank axle.*
Dar.22/2–9/3/26.**L.**
Gat.28/9–8/10/26.**L.**
Dar.19/10/27–20/3/28.**G.** *New crank axle.*
Dar.23/1–6/3/29.**L.**
Dar.9–19/7/29.**N/C.**
Dar.29/11/29–7/2/30.**G.** *Bronze axleboxes.*
Dar.3–19/6/30.**N/C.**
Dar.2/3–3/5/32.**G.** *Steam brake.*
Dar.30/8–29/9/32.**H.**
Dar.12/5–16/6/33.**H.**
Dar.9–28/8/33.**N/C.**
Dar.16/1–18/5/34.**G.** *New cylinders.*
Dar.1/11–6/12/34.**N/C.** *8 wheel tender.*
Dar.8/11/35–18/3/36.**G.** *New cylinders and vacuum brake.*
Dar.24/3–14/4/36.**N/C.** *Valves re-set.*
Dar.6/4/37 – *Not repaired.*

BOILERS:
1447.
1448 (ex2401) 7/2/30.
1602 (ex2403) 29/9/32.
1606 (ex2401) 16/6/33.
1602 (ex2403) 18/3/36.

SHEDS:
Gateshead.
York 7/5/34.

CONDEMNED:
13/4/37.
Tender returned to Doncaster 16/8/37, engine cut–up on 28/8/37. Boiler made Stationery Boiler No. 7112 to serve as Bosh Tank steam supply until it ceased work in May 1939 and was then cut–up.

2401
CITY OF KINGSTON UPON HULL.

Darlington.

Booked to traffic 30/12/1922.

REPAIRS:
Dar.17–19/9/23.**L.**
Dar.18/10/24–29/1/25.**G.**
Gat.16–18/6/26.**L.**
Gat.29–31/12/36.**L.**
Dar.18/2–29/3/27.**L.**
Dar.8/4–7/11/27.**G.** *New crank axle.*
Dar.11–23/11/27.**L.**
Gat.6–25/6/29.**L.**
Dar.9–17/7/29.**N/C.**
Dar.29/8–8/11/29.**G.** *Bronze axleboxes.*
Dar.11–13/2/30.**N/C.**
Dar.28/7–6/8/30.**N/C.**
Dar.7–21/1/31.**N/C.**
Dar.2/2–12/3/31.**N/C.**
Dar.9/7–19/8/31.**N/C.**
Dar.19/8–5/11/31.**G.** *New cylinders and steam brake.*
Dar.6/12/32–17/2/33.**H.**
Dar.27/10–15/12/33.**G.**
Dar.12/9–9/10/34.**N/C.** *8 wheel tender.*
Dar.1–18/7/35.**N/C.**
Dar.13/1/36 – *Not repaired.*

BOILERS:
1448.
1606 (ex2404) 8/11/29.
1447 (ex2402) 17/2/33.

SHEDS:
Gateshead.
York 9/2/34.

CONDEMNED:
3/7/36.
Tender returned to Doncaster 16/6/36, engine cut–up 15/8/36, boiler 22/8/36.

2402
CITY OF YORK.

Darlington.

To traffic 11/3/24.

REPAIRS:
Dar.2–19/7/24.**L.**
Dar.3/11/25–30/3/26.**G.** *New crank axle.*

Gat.10–25/3/27.**L.**
Gat.15–29/11/27.**L.**
Gat.30/12/27–2/2/28.**L.**
Dar.11/9–7/12/28.**G.**
Dar.21–28/12/28.**L.**
Dar.28/1–2/4/30.**G.** *New crank axle and bronze axleboxes.*
Dar.26/10/31–5/1/32.**G.** *Steam brake.*
Dar.19/8–3/10/32.**L.**
Dar.25/11/32–10/1/33.**H.**
Dar.15/6–13/8/34.**G.** *8 wheel tender.*
Dar.7/9–3/10/34.**L.** *Collision damage.*
Dar.6/7/36 – *Not repaired.*

BOILERS:
1597.
1447 (ex2400) 2/4/30.
1448 (ex2400) 10/1/33.
1597 (ex2403) 13/8/34.

SHEDS:
Gateshead.
York 13/8/34.

CONDEMNED:
25/7/36.
Tender returned to Doncaster 7/9/36, engine cut–up 29/8/36, boiler 5/9/36.

2403
CITY OF DURHAM.

Darlington.

To traffic 24/3/24.

REPAIRS:
Dar.29/7–18/8/24.**L.**
Dar.11/11/25–29/6/26.**G.** *New crank axle.*
Dar.30/11–15/12/36.**L.**
Gat.26/10–21/12/27.**L.**
Gat.23–25/1/28.**L.**
Dar.6/2–16/5/29.**G.**
Gat.13/2–1/3/30.**L.**
Dar.6/3–25/6/30.**G.** *Bronze axleboxes.*
Dar.14–20/8/30.**N/C.**
Dar.16/6–9/7/31.**L.**
Dar.31/12/31–19/2/32.**G.** *Steam brake.*
Dar.2–4/2/33.**N/C.**
Dar.2–13/3/33.**N/C.**
Dar.28/9–7/11/33.**G.**
Dar.15–23/6/34.**N/C.**
Dar.19/10–19/11/34.**N/C.** *8 wheel tender.*

Dar.29/7–18/10/35.**G.** *Vacuum brake.*
Dar.6–17/3/36.**N/C.**
Dar.22/9–27/10/36.**N/C.**
Dar.4/5/37.*Not repaired.*

BOILERS:
1602.
1597 (ex2402) 19/2/32.
1602 (ex2400) 7/11/33.
1448 (ex2402) 18/10/35.

SHEDS:
Gateshead.
York 26/4/34.

CONDEMNED:
21/5/37.
Tender returned to Doncaster 13/8/37, engine cut–up 5/2/38, boiler 25/6/38.

2404
CITY OF RIPON.

Darlington.

To traffic 25/3/24.

REPAIRS:
Dar.14–25/4/24.**L.**
Dar.16/6–2/7/24.**L.**
Gat.19–26/7/24.**L.**
Dar.30/12/25–25/1/26.**L.**
Dar.26/4–29/10/26.**G.**
Dar.5–17/11/26.**L.**
Gat.19/10–21/12/27.**L.**
Dar.26/4–26/9/29.**G.** *Bronze axleboxes.*
Gat.1–4/4/30.**L.** *Valves re-set.*
Gat.11–30/4/30.**L.**
Gat.9–13/6/30.**L.** *Valves re-set.*
Dar.6/5–21/8/31.**G.**
Gat.26–30/10/31.**L.**
Dar.15–31/8/32.**N/C.**
Dar.24/1–28/4/33.**G.** *Steam brake.*
Dar.6/7–1/9/33.**H.**
Dar.29/6–9/7/34.**N/C.**
Dar.5/10/34–30/1/35.**H.** *8 wheel tender.*
Dar.4/11/35–24/1/36.**G.** *Vacuum brake.*
Dar.25/1–6/2/36.**N/C.**
Dar.28/2–18/3/36.**N/C.**

BOILERS:
1606.
7791 (ex2569) 26/9/29.

2404 Continued

SHEDS:	*CONDEMNED:*	Tender returned to
Gateshead.	6/2/37.	Doncaster 20/3/37, engine
York 7/11/34.		cut–up 5/6/37, boiler sent to
		Doncaster 17/3/37.

2401 moved to York shed on 9th February 1934, and went to works on 12th September, for a change to a bigger tender. On Saturday 6th June it is about to run through Grantham with a 14 coach load on the Norwegian boat express. The train is on its way to Tyne Commission Quay, 2401 working it from Kings Cross to York.

The official photograph of the LNER–built trio. These differed from the North Eastern pair by having outside, instead of inside bearings, for the carrying axle under the cab. The piping for the steam reversing gear is noticeable, also the provision of three safety valves, and the absence of lifting holes in the frames.

2403 on 8th June 1929 at York shed, having worked in from Newcastle. At rail level, below the figure 4 on the cab, the striker for the Raven fog signalling apparatus can be seen. All five were so equipped until that system ceased to be used, from the end of October 1933.

This was *not* a posed photograph, despite the unlikelihood of getting the three LNER built engines all into the same picture. Neither Gateshead nor York shed had a long enough 'table to turn them, but at both locations convenient triangles existed for the purpose. So, normally, they were stabled outside between duties, and at Gateshead shed from left to right, are 2403, 2404 and 2402.

2403 had Westinghouse brake equipment removed in February 1932, and here in 1933 it is approaching Darlington with an express meat train for London. In their later years, both Gateshead and York sheds made good revenue earning use of the Raven 4–6–2s on perishables, as well as on passenger trains.

After less than three months, the cab sides were altered to a more orthodox style, and large smoke deflectors have been added, to which the nameplates were transferred. Here on 12th August 1946 it is about to leave Kings Cross on one of that shed's turns. The hinged discs fitted to indicate the class of train being worked have already lost face, with reversion to the long-standing and effective use of oil lamps.

THOMPSON A1/1

4470
GREAT NORTHERN.

Rebuilt Doncaster from
Gresley A1.

To traffic 25/9/45.

REPAIRS:
Don.2–6/10/45.**L.**
Don.2–13/12/45.**L.**
Don.20–21/1/46.**L.**
Don.26/2–6/3/46.**L.**
Don.16–21/5/46.**L.**
Don.5–11/7/46.**L.**
Don.19–25/9/46.**L.**
Don.28/3–16/5/47.**G.**
Don.18–21/6/47.**L.**
Don.11/8–1/10/48.**G.**
Don.15/9/49–6/1/50.**G.**
Don.3–11/5/50.**C/L.**
Don.2–21/6/50.**C/L.**
Don.19/4–18/5/51.**H/I.**
Don.20/11–4/12/51.**C/L.**
Don.20/7–21/8/52.**G.**
Don.25/11/53–13/1/54.**G.**
Don.15/12/54–26/1/55.**C/L.**
Don.24/2–18/4/55.**G.**
Don.20–22/4/55.**N/C.**
Don.11/1–1/2/56.**N/C.**
Don.7/8–8/9/56.**C/L.**
Don.18–20/9/56.**N/C.**
Don.7–18/1/57.**N/C.**
Don.15/4–31/5/57.**G.**
Don.24/9–8/10/57.**C/L.**
Don.20/2–5/3/58.**N/C.**
Don.2–19/4/58.**C/L.**
Don.15/9–8/10/58.**C/H.**
Don.4/5–17/6/59.**G.**
Don.21/3/60.**N/C.**
Don.5–14/7/60.**N/C.**
Don.7/12/60–2/2/61.**G.**

BOILERS:
9487 (New)6/10/45.
9031 (ex60016) 6/1/50.
*9031 Renumbered 29288
18/5/51.*
29275 (ex60016) 21/8/52.
29329 (New) 31/5/57.
29275 (ex60002) 17/6/59.
29332 (ex60015) 2/2/61.

SHEDS:
Doncaster.
Kings Cross 7/10/45.
Gateshead 24/7/47.
Haymarket 2/9/47.
Kings Cross 13/9/47.
New England 4/6/50.
Grantham 9/9/51.
Kings Cross 15/9/57.
Doncaster 13/10/57.

RENUMBERED:
No.113. 9/10/46.
No.60113. 1/10/48.

CONDEMNED:
19/11/62.
Cut–up Doncaster works
2/63.

The rebuilt Gresley Pacific in Doncaster works yard, about to have its first fire lit. Note the shallow cab sides, absence of smoke deflectors, straight nameplate on smokebox, the change to left–hand drive, and removal of redundant guard irons on frame.

Successively No.113 and then 60113, almost the whole of its useful work was limited to the ex–GN main line. South of Grantham, on 15th August 1959, the engine has the combined York and Hull morning express to London. Note alteration to chimney, name surmounted by GNR armorial, and fitting of BR Automatic Warning System.

After running-in, 3698 returned to Darlington to be fitted with electric lighting equipment, the power being derived from this axle-mounted Metropolitan–Vickers alternator. The top lamp iron had a hinged disc attached, but loose discs were provided as markers for the class of train being worked, on the buffer beam irons. All four A2/1 engines first had this Group Standard 6-wheel tender, originally ordered for them when they were to be built as class V2 engines.

THOMPSON A2/1

3696
HIGHLAND CHIEFTAIN
from 5/47.

Darlington 1930.

To traffic 13/5/44.

REPAIRS:
Dar.4–28/7/44.**L.**
Dar.28/8–2/9/44.**N/C.**
Dar.10/10–7/11/44.**L.**
Don.10–28/3/45.**L.**
Dar.4–28/6/45.**L.** *Electric lighting fitted.*
Don.26/10–24/12/45.**H.** *8 wheel tender.*
Don.18–21/11/46.**L.**
Dar.29/3–31/5/47.**G.**
Dar.19/8–4/9/47.**L.**
Dar.14/10–28/11/47.**L.**
Dar.11/8–29/10/48.**G.**
Dar.17/12/48–15/1/49.**L.**
Don.10/8–12/10/49.**G.**
Don.25/8–9/10/50.**C/L.**
Don.24/5–4/7/51.**G.**
Don.18/8–24/9/52.**H/I.**
Don.4–21/8/53.**N/C.**
Don.6/1–1/2/54.**C/L.**
Hay.9/2–2/3/54.**C/L.**
Don.23/7–26/8/54.**G.**
Don.31/8–3/9/54.**N/C.**
Don.4/1–15/2/56.**G.**
Don.16/5–2/6/56.**C/L.**
Don.3–16/7/56.**C/L.**
Don.29/8–16/10/57.**G.**
Don.15–21/11/57.**C/L.**
Don.23/11/57–1/1/58.**C/L.**
Don.5–9/8/58.**C/L.**
Don.28/9–1/10/58.**C/L.**
Don.6–12/3/59.**N/C.**
Don.10/11–16/12/59.**G.**
Don.21–24/12/59.**N/C.**
Don.24/11/60 – *Not repaired.*

BOILERS:
3475.
29371 (ex60869) 4/7/51.
29355 (ex60509) 16/10/57.
29371 (ex60510) 16/12/59.

SHEDS:
Darlington.
Heaton 8/6/44.
Kings Cross 16/11/44.
Haymarket 15/12/49.
St Margarets 13/7/60.

RENUMBERED:
507 12/5/46.
60507 29/10/48.

CONDEMNED:
12/12/60.
Cut–up Doncaster Works.

3697
DUKE OF ROTHESAY
from 1/47.

Darlington 1933.

To traffic 30/6/44.

REPAIRS:
Dar.1–3/8/44.**N/C.**
Dar.8–23/8/44.**L.**
Dar.25/8–13/9/44.**L.**
Dar.20–21/9/44.**N/C.**
Dar.13–22/11/44.**N/C.**
Don.3–10/2/45.**L.**
Don.2–23/5/45.**L.**
Dar.7/1–2/3/46.**H.**
Dar.9/11/46–17/1/47.**L.**
Dar.3/5–12/7/47.**G.**
Dar.17/11/47–6/2/48.**H.**
Dar.1/3–26/5/48.**L.**
Don.27/7–24/9/48.**G.** *After derailment.*
Don.1–15/6/49.**C/L.** *8 wheel tender.*
Don.10/5–23/6/50.**G.**
Don.24/3–25/4/52.**G.**
Don.17/3–2/4/53.**C/L.**
Don.25/8–8/10/53.**G.**
Don.5–9/8/54.**N/C.**
Don.8/3–6/4/55.**G.**
Don.3–11/10/55.**N/C.**
Don.7–16/3/56.**C/L.**
Don.11/1–16/2/57.**G.**
Don.26/11–4/12/57.**N/C.**
Don.4–14/2/58.**N/C.**
Don.30/6–9/7/58.**N/C.**
Don.31/12/58–12/2/59.**G.**
Don.20/2/61 – *Not repaired.*

BOILERS:
3480.
29406 (ex60509) 25/4/52.
29417 (ex60850) 16/2/57.
29406 (ex60509) 12/2/59.

SHEDS:
Darlington.
Kings Cross 25/11/44.
Gorton 10/2/45.
Kings Cross 28/3/45.
New England 4/6/50.

RENUMBERED:
508 20/7/46.
E508 6/2/48.
60508 26/5/48.

CONDEMNED:
20/2/61.
Cut–up Doncaster Works.

3698
WAVERLEY from 10/46.

Darlington 1944.

To traffic 15/11/44.

REPAIRS:
Dar.28/12/44–27/2/45.**L.** *Electric lighting fitted.*
Dar.2–5/3/45.**N/C.**
Cow.7–14/7/45.**L.**
Dar.15/10/45–24/1/46.**L.** *Reverse indicator plate and brake gear alteration.*
Dar.29/1–2/2/46.**N/C.**
Dar.10/4–2/5/46.**L.**
Dar.19/8–26/10/46.**H.** *8 wheel tender.*
Dar.16/1–1/3/47.**L.**
Cow.11–14/10/47.**L.**
Dar.4/6–18/8/46.**G.**
Cow.14–18/12/48.**L.**
Dar.22/1–25/2/49.**C/L.**
Don.12–27/5/49.**C/L.**
Don.14/4–2/6/50.**G.**
Don.8–14/6/50.**N/C.**
Don.14/3–13/4/51.**C/L.**
Don.27/11–27/12/51.**G.**
Don.10–28/7/52.**N/C.**
Don.31/12/52–4/2/53.**H/I.**
Don.8/12/53–19/1/54.**C/H.**
After derailment at Goswick 28/10/53.
Don.4–19/5/54.**N/C.**
Don.5/7–9/8/54.**H/I.**
Don.20/10–3/11/54.**C/L.**
Don.6–25/10/55.**C/L.**
Don.19/12/55–26/1/56.**G.**
Don.17/5–20/6/57.**G.**
Don.26/3–10/4/58.**C/L.**
Don.4/11–18/12/58.**G.**
Don.16/12/59–26/1/60.**C/L.**
Don.12/7/60 – *Not repaired.*

BOILERS:
3485.
29355 (ex60507) 27/12/51.
29406 (ex60508) 20/6/57.
29349 (ex60510) 18/12/58.

SHEDS:
Darlington 17/11/44.
Haymarket 14/3/45.
Aberdeen Ferryhill 4/9/49.
Haymarket 25/9/49.

RENUMBERED:
509 2/5/46.
60509 6/8/48.

CONDEMNED:
15/8/60.
Cut–up Doncaster Works.

3699
ROBERT THE BRUCE
from 4/48.

Darlington 1950.

To traffic 13/1/45.

REPAIRS:
Dar.23/1–7/2/45.**N/C.**
Dar.22–24/2/45.**N/C.**
Dar.3–20/7/45.**L.** *Electric lighting fitted.*
Dar.23/4–7/6/46.**H.**
Cow.5–7/9/46.**L.**
Cow.20–21/9/46.**L.**
Cow.1–2/11/46.**L.**
Dar.29/1–8/3/47.**L.**
Dar.21/2–28/4/48.**G.**
Dar.31/12/48–27/1/49.**L.**
Don.5/8–2/9/49.**C/H.** *8 wheel tender.*
Cow.2–7/4/50.**C/L.**
Don.22/5–14/7/50.**G.**
Cow.12–17/11/51.**C/L.**
Don.24/1–29/2/52.**H/I.**
Don.6–17/2/53.**N/C.**
Don.21/4–20/5/53.**G.**
Don.28/6–4/8/54.**H/I.**
Don.12–25/7/55.**N/C.**
Don.11/6–31/7/56.**G.**
Don.22/10–27/11/57.**G.**
Don.31/1–5/2/58.**N/C.**
Don.2–7/7/58.**C/L.**
Don.11–22/8/58.**N/C.**
Don.15/6–24/7/59.**G.**
Don.17/10/60 – *Not repaired.*

BOILERS:
3494 *Renumbered 29397 29/2/52.*
29349 (ex60846) 20/5/53.
29371 (ex60507) 27/11/57.
29417 (ex60508) 24/7/59.

SHEDS:
Darlington.
Haymarket 1/3/49.
Aberdeen Ferryhill 4/9/49.
Haymarket 25/9/49.
St Margarets 13/7/60.

RENUMBERED:
510 7/6/46.
60510 28/4/48.

CONDEMNED:
21/11/60.
Cut–up Doncaster Works.

WORKS CODES:– Cow – Cowlairs. Dar – Darlington. Don – Doncaster. Gat – Gateshead. Hay – Haymarket Shed. Inv – Inverurie.
REPAIR CODES:– **C/H** – Casual Heavy. **C/L** – Casual Light. **G** – General. **H** – Heavy. **H/I** – Heavy Intermediate. **L** – Light. **L/I** – Light Intermediate. **N/C** – Non–Classified.

60509 had been 3698, then 509 from 2nd May 1946, and from its first heavy repair, in October 1946, underwent appreciable changes to its original guise. The small deflectors on each side of the chimney had proved no more useful than they had been on the A3 2751 *HUMORIST* eight years ago, so they were replaced by this large type. Nameplates were affixed then, and a change to a new 8–wheel tender also took place. When ex–works on 2nd June 1950, as seen here, all the electric lighting equipment had been removed, for any running in reverse tended to unscrew the alternator, which thereupon dropped off the axle(!). Normal irons for use with oil lamps were then fitted.

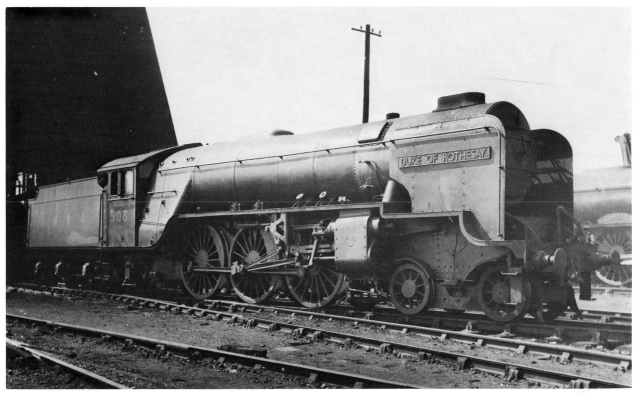

No.508 superseded 3697 from 20th July 1946, and was altered to the large smoke deflectors in January 1947, when it was also named and fitted with plates. Until December 1949 the four engines were allocated in pairs to the Southern and Scottish Areas but all four were given Scottish names. The Metropolitan–Vickers electric lighting set ordered for 3697 was never fitted, and was used instead for Thompson's rebuild of A1 No.4470.

At a heavy repair, from which it was ex–Darlingtion in February 1948, the British Railways E prefix was added to No.508, but out from a light repair on 26th May 1948 the number had become 60508. Despite both works visits, the tender still carried LNER, for here is the engine on 17th June 1948, leaving Grantham on a Leeds to Kings Cross express. About 6 a.m. on the following 17th July, No 60508 came to grief by derailment near New Southgate at around 70 mph, whilst working the 7.50 p.m. from Edinburgh to Kings Cross. The coupling parted and the engine, with tender, broke away from the train. Turning on to their sides, both slid a full 100 yards further. Passenger casualties were light but the fireman was killed. The cause, it was concluded, was a track deficiency in the Barnet tunnel, through which the train had just passed. Despite the damage to the motion, and to the right hand cab side, the smoke deflector (and nameplate on it) came out almost unscathed. The subsequent general repair took almost two months to complete, and was done by Doncaster, despite Darlington's responsibility for the A2/1 class.

60507 at Haymarket shed, to which it was consigned when Kings Cross shed no longer needed it. During the 1950s all four had the 'tin' chimneys replaced by a normal casting, adapted to suit the double blastpipe. 60507's tender continued to differ slightly from the other three in that it had handrails of matching height to those on the cab and, albeit painted over, it kept the stainless steel strip inherited from its first coupling to the bombed A4 (see *Volume Two*).

After its accident 60508 continued on main line work from Kings Cross; on the departure of 60507 to the Scottish Region, Kings Cross shed was left with only a single A2/1, so on 4th June 1950 60508 was hived off to New England, to work on secondary expresses and on fast goods trains. Here at Knebworth in 1959 on an up parcels, it shows the final condition attained at its last general repair, in February 1959. The BR type of Automatic Warning System had been fitted, but it still kept the special lamp irons suited to the electric lamps, which it never got.

60510 at Inverkeithing on an Edinburgh to Aberdeen express, after it had changed to 8-wheel tender in September 1949. After British Railways took over, the original plain sided chimney was fitted with a beading around the rim.

Originally introduced as 2–8–2s in 1934 and 1936, to eliminate the wasteful need for two engines on the heavy expresses between Edinburgh and Aberdeen, Nos.2001 – 2006 were rebuilt to 4–6–2s by Thompson. The many defects suffered by the 2–8–2s, Thompson had claimed, rendered rebuilding of the P2 class necessary. His Pacific version, however, turned out to have just as many drawbacks, albeit different ones. 2005 was done first, in January 1943, and assessed for more than a year; from April to December 1944, the same treatment was given to the other five. Under the 1943 scheme, Nos. 2001 – 2006 were to have been renumbered 990 – 995, but in May 1946 this was changed to 501 – 506, and they were also accorded green livery, 502 got the new style when ex-Cowlairs on 29th March 1947 and by then shaded transfers had been superseded by painted Gill Sans characters, which did not have shading applied.

THOMPSON A2/2

2001
COCK O' THE NORTH.

Doncaster rebuilt from P2.

To traffic 14/9/44.

REPAIRS:
Cow.22/9–6/10/45.**L.**
Don.30/3–4/5/46.**G.**
Cow.25/5–15/6/46.**L.** *Green painting for exhibition in Edinburgh.*
Cow.12/11/46–4/7/47**H.**
Cow.29–30/1/48.**L.**
Cow.23/2–9/4/49.**H/I.**
Don.2/1–21/2/50.**G.**
Don.5/1–16/2/51.**H/I.**
Don.19–21/3/51. *Special exam after Balby bridge accident.*
Don.17/9–24/10/52.**G.**
Don.2/4/53.*Weigh.*
Don.12/6–17/7/53.**C/L.**
Don.29/10–7/11/53.**N/C.**
Don.18–25/2/54.**N/C.**
Don.15–19/3/54.**N/C.**
Don.1–7/4/54.**N/C.**
Don.12–20/5/54.**N/C.**
Don.18/8–28/9/54.**G.**
Don.29/11–10/12/54.**C/L.**
Don.8/8–28/9/56.**G.**
Don.11–19/12/57.**N/C.**
Don.14–22/3/58.**N/C.**
Don.5–12/6/58.**N/C.**
Don.17/9–23/10/58.**G.**
Don.10–12/2/59.**N/C.**
Don.22/1/60 – *Not repaired.*

BOILERS:
8797 (ex2002).
8797 renumbered 29771 16/2/51.
29837 (ex60115) 24/10/52.
29807 (ex60161) 28/9/54.
29876 (ex60515) 28/9/56.
29807 (ex60530) 23/10/58.

SHEDS:
Haymarket.
Aberdeen Ferryhill 29/10/44.
Haymarket 4/9/49.
York 27/11/49.
Neville Hill 27/11/50.
York 17/12/50.

RENUMBERED:
501 11/8/46.
60501 22/5/48.

CONDEMNED:
8/2/60.
Cut–up Doncaster Works.

2002
EARL MARISCHAL.

Doncaster rebuilt from P2.

To traffic 23/6/44.

REPAIRS:
Cow.2–6/2/45.**L.**
Cow.16–28/4/45.**L.**
Cow.12–15/5/45.**L.**
Cow.10–13/9/45.**L.**
Cow.10/10–24/11/45.**H.**
Inv.13/12/45.*Weigh.*
Inv.20–22/1/46.**L.**
Cow.16–26/2/46.**L.**
Cow.18–19/9/46.**L.**
Cow.13–21/12/46.**L.**
Cow.3–5/2/47.**N/C.**
Cow.22/2–29/3/47.**L.**
Cow.7–18/7/47.**L.**
Cow.19/12/47–28/2/48.**H.**
Cow.28–30/6/48.**L.**
Cow.4–13/11/48.**L.**
Cow.11–14/1/49.**L/C.**
Inv.10–15/6/49.**N/C.**
Cow.11/8–3/9/49.**H/I.**
Don.22/1–7/3/51.**G.**
Don.12–15/3/51.**N/C.**
Don.29/9–4/11/52.**G.**
Don.3–11/3/54.**N/C.**
Don.26/8–8/10/54.**G.**
Don.3/2–1/3/56.**C/L.**
Don.19/7–31/8/56.**G.**
Don.23/9–11/10/57.**C/L.**
Don.8–20/11/57.**N/C.**
Don.2/12/58–9/1/59.**G.**
Don.25/8–24/9/59.**C/L.**
Don.26/6/61 – *Not repaired.*

BOILERS:
8934 (ex2006).
8798 (ex2004) 24/11/45.
29835 (New) 7/3/51.
29840 (ex60122) 4/11/52.
29852 (ex60123) 8/10/54.
29840 (ex60525) 31/8/56.
29867 (ex60159) 9/1/59.

SHEDS:
Aberdeen Ferryhill.
Haymarket 4/9/49.
York 27/11/49.

RENUMBERED:
502 12/5/46.
60502 30/6/48.

CONDEMNED:
3/7/61.
Cut–up Doncaster Works.

2003
LORD PRESIDENT.

Doncaster rebuilt from P2.

To traffic 17/12/44.

REPAIRS:
Don.30/12/44.**L.**
Don.17/3/45.**N/C.**
Cow.15–27/6/45.**L.**
Cow.29–31/8/45.**L.**
Cow.22/10–3/11/45.**L.**
Cow.9–12/11/45.**L.**
Inv.23/11/45.*Weigh.*
Cow.6/7–21/12/46.**H.**
Cow.27/6–12/7/47.**L.**
Cow.9/8–18/9/48.**G.**
Cow.27–30/10/48.**L.**
Cow.10–13/5/49.**N/C.**
Don.30/11–20/12/49.**C/L.**
Bogie exam after derailment.
Don.24/7–31/8/50.**G.**
Don.25–26/10/50.*Weigh.*
Don.20/2–13/3/51.**C/L.**
Don.5/3–2/4/52.**H/I.**
Don.22/4–2/5/52.**N/C.**
Don.20/11–10/12/52.**C/L.**
Don.6–23/11/53.**N/C.**
Don.21–28/1/54.**C/L.**
Don.26/5–9/6/54.**N/C.**
Don.30/12/54–4/2/55.**G.**
Don.17/10–15/11/55.**C/L.**
Don.12–27/1/56.**N/C.**
Don.4/12/56.*Weigh.*
Don.7/6–26/7/57.**G.**
Don.27/5–6/6/58.**N/C.**
Don.20/10–12/11/58.**C/L.**
Don.20/2–14/3/59.**C/L.**
Don.27/11/59 – *Not repaired.*

BOILERS:
8785 (Retained).
8785 renumbered 29772 2/4/52.
29770 (ex60504) 4/2/55.

SHEDS:
Kings Cross.
Gateshead 2/2/45.
Haymarket 20/3/45.
Kings Cross 11/4/45.
Haymarket 13/5/45.
Aberdeen Ferryhill 17/5/48.
Haymarket 26/5/48.
York 27/11/49.
Neville Hill 27/11/50.
York 17/12/50.

RENUMBERED:
503 30/6/46.
60503 18/9/48.

CONDEMNED:
27/11/59.
Cut–up Doncaster Works.

2004
MONS MEG.

Doncaster rebuilt from P2.

To traffic 3/11/44.

REPAIRS:
Cow.7–8/7/45.**N/C.**
Cow.13/8–1/9/45.**L.**
Cow.16/11–1/12/45.**L.**
Don.5/3–12/4/46.**G.**
Cow.11/7/46.*Weigh.*
Cow.3/2–14/3/47.**L.**
Cow.27–29/8/47.**L.**
Don.28/1–12/3/48.**G.**
Don.14–23/3/48.**N/C.**
Cow.22/3–30/4/49.**L/I.**
Don.9/1–26/5/50.**G.**
Don.21/8–26/9/50.**C/L.**
Don.20/3–19/4/51.**C/L.**
Don.26/11/51–9/1/52.**H/I.**
Don.3/3/52.*Weigh.*
Don.16/3–3/4/52.**N/C.**
Don.1–29/12/52.**C/L.**
Don.14/5–15/6/53.**C/L.**
Don.7/10–16/11/53.**G.**
Don.10–17/2/54.**N/C.**
Don.17/11–21/12/54.**C/L.**
Don.1/6–15/7/55.**G.**
Don.25/7–11/8/55.**N/C.**
Don.18/9–3/10/55.**N/C.**
Don.7–8/10/55.**N/C.**
Don.12/10/55.*Weigh.*
Don.25/11/55–10/1/56.**N/C.**
Don.24/1–12/2/57.**C/L.**
Don.10/10–16/11/57.**G.**
Don.19–21/11/57.**N/C.**
Don.16–25/7/58.**C/L.**
Don.12–19/6/59.**N/C.**
Don.22/8–2/10/59.**G.**
Don.23/1/61 – *Not repaired.*

BOILERS:
8771 (ex2001).
8771 renumbered 29770 26/9/50.
29771 (ex60501) 16/11/53.

SHEDS:
Haymarket.
New England 9/1/50.

RENUMBERED:
504 30/6/46.
E504 12/3/48.
60504 23/3/48.

CONDEMNED:
23/1/61.
Cut–up Doncaster Works.

WORKS CODES:– Cow – Cowlairs. Dar – Darlington. Don – Doncaster. Gat – Gateshead. Hay – Haymarket Shed. Inv – Inverurie.

REPAIR CODES:– **C/H** – Casual Heavy. **C/L** – Casual Light. **G** – General. **H** – Heavy. **H/I** – Heavy Intermediate. **L** – Light. **L/I** – Light Intermediate. **N/C** – Non–Classified.

2005

THANE OF FIFE. Without name from rebuilding until re–fitted 6/6/44.

Doncaster rebuilt from P2.

To traffic 18/1/43.

REPAIRS:
Cow.2–6/3/44.**L.**
Cow.17/3–3/4/44.**L.**
Cow.1–6/6/44.**L.**
Cow.8/8–14/9/44.**H.**
Cow.5–8/3/45.**L.**
Cow.27–30/3/45.**L.**
Cow.23/5–9/6/45.**L.**
Cow.10–14/7/45.**L.**
Cow.15–25/8/45.**L.**
Cow.4–5/9/45.**L.**
Cow.11–14/9/45.**L.**
Inv.3/10/45.**N/C.**
Inv.17/11/45.*Weigh.*
Cow.3–22/12/45.**L.**
Cow.9–25/4/46.**L.**
Inv.22–23/5/46.**L.**
Don.13/6–19/10/46.**G.**
Don.23/10–2/11/46.**N/C.**
Cow.5/12/46.*Weigh.*
Cow.12–29/3/47.**L.**
Cow.23/4–5/6/48.**G.**
Cow.19–22/4/49.**N/C.**
Cow.2–4/8/49.**N/C.**
Cow.9–19/11/49.**N/C.**
Don.24/4–13/6/50.**G.**
Don.20–22/6/50.**N/C.**
Don.27/3–24/4/51.**C/L.**
Don.29/1–7/3/52.**G.**
Don.25/3–8/4/52.**N/C.**
Don.9–24/7/52.**C/L.**
Don.22/9–11/11/52.**C/L.**
Don.5/8–2/9/53.**N/C.**
Don.5/10/53–15/1/54.**G.**
Don.19–22/1/54.**N/C.**
Don.30/8–18/10/55.**G.**
Don.17/1–8/2/57.**C/L.**
Don.1/8–20/9/57.**G.**
Don.22–25/9/57.**N/C.**
Don.24–29/10/57.**N/C.**
Don.5/12/57–24/1/58.**N/C.**
Don.10–18/6/58.**N/C.**
Don.5–18/3/59.**C/L.**
Don.17–23/4/59.**N/C.**
Don.19/8–4/9/59.**C/L.**
Don.10/11/59 – *Not repaired.*

BOILERS:
8799 (Retained).
29872 (New) 7/3/52.
29820 (ex60154) 15/1/54.
29826 (ex60149) 18/10/55.
29786 (ex60520) 20/9/57.

SHEDS:
Doncaster.
Haymarket 3/4/43.
New England 30/12/49.

RENUMBERED:
994 25/4/46.
505 12/5/46.
60505 5/6/48.

CONDEMNED:
10/11/59.
Cut–up Doncaster Works.

2006

WOLF OF BADENOCH. Name removed at rebuilding, but re–fitted 4/6/44.

Doncaster rebuilt from P2.

To traffic 15/4/44.

REPAIRS:
Cow.19–21/6/44.**L.**
Cow.15/7–16/8/44.**L.**
Cow.17–21/10/44.**L.**
Cow.27–28/11/44.**N/C.**
Cow.11–20/3/45.**L.**
Inv.17–18/4/45.**N/C.**
Cow.10/5/45.**N/C.**
Inv.25/6/45.**N/C.**
Cow.20/8–12/9/45.**H.**
Cow.25/9/45.**N/C.**
Inv.19/10/45.*Weigh. After derailment at Craigentinny.*
Cow.8–17/1/46.**L.**
Cow.4–18/9/46.**L.**
Cow.3/1–18/10/47.**G.**
Cow.14–18/12/48.**L.**
Cow.19/5–17/6/49.**H/I.**
Cow.14/7/49.**N/C.**
Don.4/6–28/7/50.**G.**
Don.29/4–9/6/52.**G.**
Don.30/9–29/10/52.**N/C.**
Don.2–21/1/53.**C/L.**
Don.11/11–9/12/53.**N/C.**
Don.25/2–3/3/54.**N/C.**
Don.26/5–9/7/54.**H/I.**
Don.17/1–14/2/55.**C/L.**
Don.3/11–3/12/55.**C/L.**
Don.18/1–7/2/56.**C/L.**
Don.24/2–27/3/56.**C/L.**
Don.4–19/7/56.**C/L.**
Don.10/9–3/10/56.**C/L.**
Don.13/11/56–5/1/57.**G.**
Don.24/5–11/6/57.**C/L.**
Don.23/9–22/10/57.**C/H.**
Don.2–10/1/58.**N/C.**
Don.6–17/6/58.**N/C.**
Don.7–21/8/58.**N/C.**
Don.22/9–2/10/58.**N/C.**
Don.15–21/11/58.**N/C.**
Don.5/1–27/2/59.**G.**
Don.18–25/9/59.**N/C.**
Don.4/4/61 – *Not repaired.*

BOILERS:
8796 (ex2003).
29867 (ex60119) 9/6/52.
29847 (ex60117) 5/1/57.
29840 (ex60502) 27/2/59.

SHEDS:
Haymarket.
Aberdeen Ferryhill 8/4/49.
Haymarket 15/5/49.
New England 20/11/49.

RENUMBERED:
506 30/6/46.
60506 18/12/48.

CONDEMNED:
4/4/61.
Cut–up Doncaster Works.

2001 at Burntisland in July 1946, with one of its regular duties, the Aberdeen to London express meat train as far as Edinburgh. It was the only A2/2 to be painted green whilst still having its original number.

When rebuilt to 4–6–2s, all six again worked in Scotland until the end of November 1949, when five of the new Peppercorn A1 class made them redundant. Three were transferred to York, and the other three to New England, for work on secondary expresses and on fast goods trains. Working from Kings Cross to Peterborough on 15th April 1950, No. 60505 still had a tender lettered LNER.

After Nationalisation, when the original shortened boilers were reaching the end of their useful life (three were cut up in 1951/2) authority was given for the A2/2 class to receive boilers intended for A2/3s and Peppercorn A1 Pacifics. To do so meant the cutting back of the cab front, to clear the safety valves, and the boiler cleading plates to be altered to suit a dome position 11⁷⁄₈ inches further forward. Boilers from A2/3 engines had a circular dome, but when used on the A2/2 class, the latter's banjo–type cover was retained. Here we are fortunate to have visual evidence of a circular dome in use on an A2/2. No.60505, at Doncaster works in November 1959, is in the first stages of scrapping.

MONS MEG, on completing its general repair of **12th March 1948**, was in LNER livery but displayed its new ownership, and its number had the E prefix to indicate the Region responsible for maintenance. Application of the prefix lasted less than eight weeks, and by its release to traffic on 23rd March, *MONS MEG* had been back into the Paint Shop for E504 to be updated to 60504.

Typical of the work this class did in England, demonstrated at York on 3rd August 1957, when that shed's 60503 has just taken over one of the express container trains of meat, to work it to London. The wedge-fronted cab survived to withdrawal on 60503 because it was always able to be fitted with one of the original boilers.

THANE OF FIFE ran for only seventeen days numbered 994, so we are very fortunate to have visual evidence of it doing so. Here in Edinburgh Waverley it is about to leave from the west end on a stopping train, about late April in 1946. It was then in black paint, without lining, and had only the wartime NE on its tender.

This view of 60506 at Haymarket shed is included to show the panel of lining on the rear of the tender, and the unshaded lettering. Its green painting was applied by Cowlairs at the October 1947 general repair, but the numbering was changed from 506 to 60506 at a light repair in mid–December 1948. Cowlairs was then using the incorrect style of figure 6, which should not have had this curved over tail.

Although long recognised as failing to serve their intended purpose, the small smoke deflectors on the smokebox were never taken off the A2/2 engines. This 9th July 1958 view of 60505 at Grantham shed also shows the sheet metal chimney to have been retained, and this was only changed to the cast type as late as March 1959. The forward dome position of an A2/3 boiler is clearly evident, as is retention of banjo–shaped cover.

60504 also managed to keep one of the original boilers, and its wedge–fronted cab, to withdrawal. Here on 3rd May 1958, this express of only five coaches and a van, at New Southgate, is a meagre load for an engine of its potential. In April 1951 it was the first A2/2 to change to a cast chimney; four others acquired one from 1954 to 1958, but 60506 was never so fitted.

No.500 brought together Thompson's various ideas on Pacific design, and he gave it class A2. From 22nd April 1947 Peppercorn changed that to A2/3. It was the 2000th engine built by Doncaster and in view of his impending retirement, the LNER Board allowed it to be named *EDWARD THOMPSON*. At Nottingham Victoria on 29th May 1946, with plates covered, it is going to Marylebone for the official naming ceremony.

THOMPSON A2/3

500
EDWARD THOMPSON.

Doncaster 2000.

To traffic 24/5/46.

REPAIRS:
Don.5–7/6/46.**N/C.**
Don.21–22/6/46.**N/C.**
Don.5–6/7/46.**N/C.**
Don.22/7/46.**N/C.**
Don.7–8/8/46.**C/L.**
Don.21–23/8/46.**C/L.**
Don.21–24/9/46.**N/C.**
Dar.2–25/10/46.**L.** *Special overhaul and fittings for Dynamometer Car test.*
Don.29–30/4/47.*Weigh.*
Don.17/1–26/2/48.**G.**
Don.1–10/3/48.**N/C.**
Don.2/8–7/10/49.**G.**
Don.9–31/3/50.**C/H.**
Don.12–26/5/50.**C/L.**
Don.29/5–13/7/51.**G.**
Don.5–13/2/52.**N/C.**
Don.25/11/52–1/1/53.**H/I.**
Don.29/4–18/6/53.**C/H.**
Don.21/10–24/11/54.**G.**
Don.22/5–5/7/56.**G.**
Don.6–15/12/56.**N/C.**
Don.7/3–10/4/58.**G.**
Don.23/2–6/3/59.**N/C.**
Don.26/8–29/9/59.**C/L.**
Don.12/2–18/3/60.**G.**
Don.23/4–6/5/60.**C/L.**
Don.15/2–30/3/62.**G.**
Don.16/10–2/11/62.**N/C.**
Don.22/4–16/5/63.**C/L.**

BOILERS:
3677.
29783 (ex60514) 13/7/51.
29781 (ex60524) 24/11/54.
29790 (ex60523) 5/7/56.
29788 (ex60522) 10/4/58.
29790 (ex60537) 18/3/60.
29819 (ex60138) 30/3/62.

SHEDS:
Gateshead.
Kings Cross 7/6/46.
Doncaster 20/7/46.
Kings Cross 12/9/46.
New England 4/6/50.

RENUMBERED:
E**500** 26/2/48.
60500 7/10/49.

CONDEMNED:
16/6/63.
Into Doncaster Works for cut–up 2/9/63.

511
AIRBORNE.

Doncaster 2002.

To traffic 20/7/46.

REPAIRS:
Don.23–24/8/46.**L.**
Dar.6/2/47.*Weigh.*
Dar.7–23/8/47.**L.**
Don.1/3–16/4/48.**G.**
Don.21/11–23/12/49.**G.**
Don.18/7–21/8/51.**G.**
Don.12/11–16/12/52.**G.**
Don.16/3–12/4/54.**C/L.**
Don.23/11–23/12/54.**G.**
Don.5/3–14/4/56.**G.**
Don.9/1–7/2/58.**G.**
Don.28/8–4/9/58.**N/C.**
A.W.S. fitted.
Don.15/7–18/8/59.**G.**
Don.22/8–7/10/61.**G.**

BOILERS:
3690.
29847 (ex60137) 21/8/51.
29835 (ex60502) 16/12/52.
29851 (ex60137) 23/12/54.
29818 (ex60145) 7/2/58.
29857 (ex60120) 18/8/59.
29778 (ex60517) 7/10/61.

SHEDS:
Gateshead.
Heaton 8/9/46.
Tweedmouth 1/10/61.

RENUMBERED:
60511 16/4/48.

CONDEMNED:
12/11/62.
Into Doncaster Works for cut–up 30/4/63.

512
STEADY AIM.

Doncaster 2003.

To traffic 24/8/46.

REPAIRS:
Gat.18–28/10/47.**N/C.**
Don.7/2–20/3/48.**G.**
Don.20/10–12/11/48.**L.**
Don.13/12/49–6/4/50.**G.**
Don.2–22/1/51.**C/H.**
Don.8/4–14/5/52.**G.**
Don.19–22/5/52.**N/C.**
Don.19–27/2/53.**N/C.**
Don.22/12/53–23/1/54.**G.**

Don.28/9–4/11/55.**G.**
Don.15/10–16/11/57.**G.**
Don.30/6–10/7/58.**N/C.**
Don.24/8–1/9/59.**N/C.**
Don.5/12/59–9/1/60.**G.**
Don.5/6–3/8/62.**G.**
Don.16–21/8/62.**N/C.**
Don.6/9–8/10/62.**C/L.**
Don.1–18/3/63.**N/C.**

BOILERS:
3710.
29777 (ex60517) 14/5/52.
29786 (ex60516) 23/1/54.
29780 (ex60514) 4/11/55.
29829 (ex60534) 16/11/57.
29832 (ex60523) 9/1/60.
29829 (ex60522) 3/8/62.

SHEDS:
Gateshead.
Heaton 8/9/46.
York 14/12/52.
St Margarets 2/12/62.
Polmadie 15/9/63.
Dundee 14/6/65.

RENUMBERED:
60512 20/3/48.

CONDEMNED:
19/6/65.
Sold for scrap 7/65 to Motherwell Machinery & Scrap Co.

513
DANTE.

Doncaster 2004.

To traffic 31/8/46.

REPAIRS:
Don.25/7–24/9/47.**G.**
Don.17/2/48.*Weigh.*
Don.27/9–3/11/48.**G.**
Don.17/7–15/8/50.**G.**
Don.28/9–19/10/50.**C/L.**
Don.11–20/7/51.**C/L.** *After collision.*
Don.20/5–18/6/52.**G.**
Don.12–27/5/53.**N/C.**
Don.2–31/3/54.**G.** *Lipped chimney fitted.*
Don.24/8–4/10/55.**G.**
Don.6/9–10/10/56.**C/L.**
Don.24/12/56–10/1/57.**C/L.**
Don.11/12/57–11/1/58.**G.**
Don.12–20/8/58.**N/C.**
Don.23/2–2/3/59.**N/C.**
Don.7/10–13/11/59.**G.**
Don.1–9/3/60.**C/L.**

Don.24/3–1/4/60.**C/L.**
Don.18/8–6/10/61.**G.**
Don.14–24/11/61.**N/C.**
Don.3–11/12/62.**N/C.**

BOILERS:
3707.
10635 (New) 15/8/50.
10635 renumbered 29809 19/10/50.
29833 (ex60526) 18/6/52.
29809 (ex60527) 4/10/55.
29826 (ex60505) 11/1/58.
29777 (ex60525) 13/11/59.
29861 (ex60136) 6/10/61.

SHEDS:
Kings Cross.
New England 19/12/48.
Grantham 8/6/58.
New England 14/6/59.

RENUMBERED:
60513 3/11/48.

CONDEMNED:
27/4/63.
Into Doncaster Works for cut–up 1/5/63.

514
CHAMOSSAIRE.

Doncaster 2005.

To traffic 28/9/46.

REPAIRS:
Don.28/5–6/6/47.**L.**
Don.29/11/47–9/1/48.**G.**
Don.9–23/3/48.**L.**
Don.9/12/48–28/1/49.**G.**
Don.7–30/3/49.**C/L.**
Don.2/10–3/11/50.**G.**
Don.22/4–22/5/52.**G.**
Don.23/11–24/12/53.**G.**
Don.11/7–12/8/55.**G.**
Don.1/1–5/2/57.**G.**
Don.3–9/4/57.**N/C.**
Don.23/7–29/8/58.**H/I.**
Don.27/9–8/10/58.**N/C.**
Don.26/1–13/2/59.**C/L.**
Don.7–16/4/59.**C/L.**
Don.29/1–3/3/60.**C/H.**
Don.13–21/5/60.**C/L.**
Don.16/1–23/2/61.**G.**
Don.15–17/5/61.**C/L.**
Don.7–16/3/62.**N/C.**
Don.2/10–26/11/62.**C/L.**

BOILERS:
3713.
3742 (ex524) 28/1/49.

WORKS CODES:– Cow – Cowlairs. Dar – Darlington. Don – Doncaster. Gat – Gateshead. Hay – Haymarket Shed. Inv – Inverurie.
REPAIR CODES:– C/H – Casual Heavy. C/L – Casual Light. G – General. H – Heavy. H/I – Heavy Intermediate. L – Light. L/I – Light Intermediate. N/C – Non–Classified.

23

The other fourteen of the class all got names of winning racehorses, and differed from 500 through the absence of electric lighting equipment. 511 gave the first indication that use of the attractive, and clearly identifiable shaded transfers might be on the way out. Its figures and letters were in customary style, but devoid of any shading.

60515 was one of the four which, from 1952, worked from York shed for ten years, and that led to their being seen in Hull where Pacifics were not common. Here on 7th April 1954 it is about to leave Paragon station with the 9.02 a.m. to Leeds, which was a through train to Liverpool Lime Street.

3742 renumbered 29778
3/11/50.
29789 (ex60512) 22/5/52.
29780 (ex60518) 24/12/53.
29791 (ex60517) 12/8/55.
29784 (ex60519) 5/2/57.
29845 (ex60145) 23/2/61.

SHEDS:
Kings Cross.
New England 19/12/48.

RENUMBERED:
60514 23/3/48.

CONDEMNED:
29/12/62.
Into Doncaster Works for
cut–up 4/6/63.

515
SUN STREAM.

Doncaster 2006.

To traffic 19/10/46.

REPAIRS:
Don.6–14/6/47.**L.**
Don.29/7–9/8/47.**L.**
Don.21/5–25/6/48.**G.**
Dar.22–23/12/48.**N/C.**
Don.13/9–20/10/49.**G.**
Don.30/11–15/12/50.**C/L.**
Don.15/8–21/9/51.**G.**
Don.26/9–2/10/51.**N/C.**
Don.4–8/10/51.**N/C.**
Don.2/2–2/3/53.**G.**
Don.6/7–11/8/54.**G.**
Don.21/11–10/12/55.**C/L.**
Don.12–14/4/56.**N/C.**
Don.28/7–8/9/56.**G.**
Don.23/9–24/10/58.**G.**
Don.16/7–31/8/60.**G.**

BOILERS:
3715.
29851 (ex60134) 21/9/51.
29856 (ex60157) 2/3/53.
29876 (New) 11/8/54.
29845 (ex60534) 8/9/56.
29870 (ex60149) 24/10/58.
29854 (ex60522) 31/8/60.

SHEDS:
Heaton.
Gateshead 6/7/52.
York 14/12/52.

RENUMBERED:
60515 25/6/48.

CONDEMNED:
12/11/62.
Into Doncaster Works for
cut–up 9/4/63.

516
HYCILLA.

Doncaster 2007.

To traffic 2/11/46.

REPAIRS:
Don.30/10–2/12/47.**H.**
Don.19/8–8/10/48.**G.**
Don.31/1–7/6/50.**G.**
Don.2–29/1/52.**H/I.**
Don.26/1–12/2/53.**C/L.**
Don.13/10–12/11/53.**G.**
Don.18/1–18/2/55.**G.**
Don.6/6–21/7/56.**G.**
Gat.16–27/9/57.**C/L.**
Don.21/1–21/2/58.**G.**
Don.29/6–6/8/59.**G.**
Don.11–13/8/59.**N/C.**
Don.3/1–9/2/61.**G.**
Don.20/2–1/3/61.**C/L.**

BOILERS:
3720 Renumbered 29786
29/1/52.
29784 (ex60521) 12/11/53.
29783 (ex60500) 18/2/55.
29781 (ex60500) 21/7/56.
29789 (ex60521) 21/2/58.
29783 (ex60521) 6/8/59.
29841 (ex60154) 9/2/61.

SHEDS:
Heaton.
Gateshead 6/7/52.
Heaton 22/5/60.
York 12/6/60.

RENUMBERED:
60516 8/10/48.

CONDEMNED:
12/11/62.
Into Doncaster Works for
cut–up 1/4/63.

517
OCEAN SWELL.

Doncaster 2008.

To traffic 28/11/46.

REPAIRS:
Don.7/7–27/8/48.**G.**
Don.3/1–23/2/50.**G.**
Don.18/8–14/9/50.**C/L.**
Don.30/7–4/9/51.**G.**
Don.4/6–3/7/52.**C/L.**
Don.3–14/11/52.**C/L.**
Don.11/8–18/9/53.**G.**
Don.15/4–13/5/54.**C/L.**
Don.28/6–29/7/55.**G.**
Don.7/3–11/4/57.**G.**
Don.14/11/58–2/1/59.**G.**
Don.25–28/7/60.**C/L.**
Don.31/10–2/12/60.**G.**
Don.17/7–2/9/61.**C/L.**
Don.26/2–14/3/62.**C/L.**

BOILERS:
3724 Renumbered 29777

14/9/50.
29785 (ex60500) 4/9/51.
29791 (ex60511) 18/9/53.
29778 (ex60522) 29/7/55.
29791 (ex60514) 11/4/57.
29778 (ex60527) 2/1/59.
29853 (ex60530) 2/12/60.

SHEDS:
Heaton.
Tweedmouth 1/10/61.

RENUMBERED:
60517 27/8/48.

CONDEMNED:
12/11/62.
Into Doncaster Works for
cut–up 18/4/63.

518
TEHRAN.

Doncaster 2009.

To traffic 28/12/46.

REPAIRS:
Don.3–9/1/47.**N/C.**
Don.14–18/1/47.**N/C.**
Don.22/8/47.*Weigh.*
Dar.8/9/47.*Weigh.*
Don.22/9/47.*Weigh.*
Don.2/6–15/7/48.**G.**
Dar.28/7/48.*Weigh.*
Don.20/12/49–1/2/50.**G.**
Don.6–15/2/50.**N/C.**
Don.19/12/50–18/1/51.**H/I.**
Don.8–23/2/51.**C/L.**
Don.11/7–15/8/51.**C/L.**
Don.31/8–7/9/51.**N/C.**
Dar.29/9–1/10/51.**N/C.**
Don.25/8–2/10/52.**G.**
Gat.2–13/4/53.**N/C.**
Don.11/1–9/2/54.**G.** *Lipped
chimney.*
Don.31/3–6/5/55.**G.**
Don.12–29/11/55.**C/L.**
Don.6/9–5/10/56.**C/L.**
Don.8/10–15/11/57.**G.**
Don.14–23/8/58.**N/C.**
Don.25/4–28/5/59.**G.**
Don.3/1–8/2/61.**G.**

BOILERS:
3731 Renumbered 29780
18/1/51.
29790 (ex60520) 2/10/52.
29787 (ex60520) 9/2/54.
29779 (ex60523) 6/5/55.
29824 (ex60539) 15/11/57.
29830 (ex60539) 28/5/59.
29820 (ex60144) 8/2/61.

SHEDS:
Gateshead.
Heaton 25/2/60.
York 12/6/60.

RENUMBERED:
60518 15/7/48.

CONDEMNED:
12/11/62.
Into Doncaster Works for
cut–up 28/3/63.

519
HONEYWAY.

Doncaster 2010.

To traffic 1/2/47.

REPAIRS:
Don.6–15/2/47.**N/C.**
Don.17–20/6/47.**L.**
Don.15/9–22/10/48.**G.**
Don.7/6–21/7/50.**G.**
Don.14–18/5/50.**N/C.**
Don.3/4–7/5/52.**H/I.**
Don.30/11–31/12/53.**G.**
Don.21/3–27/4/55.**G.**
Don.2/11–8/12/56.**G.**
Don.17/3–25/4/58.**G.**
Don.31/10–2/12/59.**G.**
Don.29/6–4/8/61.**G.**
Don.18/12/62 – *Not
repaired.*

BOILERS:
3728 Renumbered 29788
7/5/52.
29785 (ex60517) 31/12/53.
29784 (ex60516) 27/4/55.
29782 (ex60524) 8/12/56.
29868 (ex60531) 25/4/58.
29826 (ex60513) 2/12/59.
29818 (ex60155) 4/8/61.

SHEDS:
Haymarket.
St Margarets 16/10/61.
York 2/12/62.

RENUMBERED:
60519 22/10/48.

CONDEMNED:
18/12/62.
Cut–up Doncaster Works.

520
OWEN TUDOR.

Doncaster 2011.

To traffic 29/3/47.

REPAIRS:
Don.17/7–2/8/47.**L.**
Don.18–29/8/47.**L.**
Don.8–21/10/47.**L.**
Don.12/4/48.*Weigh.*
Don.6/7–13/8/48.**G.**
Don.12/5–23/6/50.**G.**
Don.12/2/51.*Weigh.*
Don.18/2–21/3/52.**G.**

WORKS CODES:– Cow – Cowlairs. Dar – Darlington. Don – Doncaster. Gat – Gateshead. Hay – Haymarket Shed. Inv – Inverurie.

REPAIR CODES:– **C/H** – Casual Heavy. **C/L** – Casual Light. **G** – General. **H** – Heavy. **H/I** – Heavy Intermediate. **L** – Light. **L/I** – Light Intermediate. **N/C** – Non–Classified.

25

In due course, BR increased the numbering by 60000, also making minor alterations and additions. These included replacement of the sheet metal chimney by cast type, a cast numberplate fitted on the smokebox door, and installation of the BR Automatic Warning System. In their latter days, A2/3s tended to be used as mixed traffic engines, and 60514, at Newcastle Central on 21st May 1962, is working a tanker train. It was the only one never to have its chimney changed to the more attractive cast type.

Don.4/1–2/2/54.**G.**
Don.18/10–26/11/55.**G.**
Don.24/3–6/4/56.**C/L.**
Don.8–13/10/56.**N/C.**
Don.14/1–23/2/57.**G.**
Don.9/12/58–17/1/59.**G.**
Don.10/2–27/4/60.**C/L.**
Don.29/3–18/5/61.**G.**

BOILERS:
3760.
29787 (ex60515) 21/3/52.
29789 (ex60514) 2/2/54.
29786 (ex60512) 26/11/55.
29852 (ex60502) 23/2/57.
29873 (ex60114) 17/1/59.
29884 (New) 18/5/61.

SHEDS:
Doncaster.
New England 12/12/48.
Grantham 15/9/57.
New England 14/6/59.
Doncaster 10/1/60.
New England 23/9/62.

RENUMBERED:
60520 13/8/48.

CONDEMNED:
16/6/63.
Into Doncaster Works for cut–up 29/8/63.

521
WATLING STREET.

Doncaster 2012.

To traffic 8/5/47.

REPAIRS:
Don.7/4–21/5/48.**G.**
Don.9/11–15/12/49.**G.**
Don.11/6–19/7/51.**G.**
Lipped chimney.
Don.29/9–31/10/52.**G.**
Don.1/3–2/4/54.**G.**
Don.4–20/5/55.**C/L.**
Don.25/10–30/11/55.**G.**
Don.25/9–26/10/57.**G.**
Don.3–19/9/58.**N/C.**
Don.7–24/2/59.**C/L.**
Don.26/5–3/7/59.**G.**
Don.30/7–26/8/60.**C/L.**
Don.10/2–16/3/61.**G.**
Don.17/7–2/8/61.**C/L.**

BOILERS:
3765 *Renumbered 29784 19/7/51.*
29782 (ex60523) 31/10/52.
29777 (ex60512) 2/4/54.
29789 (ex60520) 30/11/55.
29783 (ex60516) 26/10/57.
29824 (ex60518) 3/7/59.
29783 (ex60516) 16/3/61.

SHEDS:
Gateshead.
Heaton 22/5/60.
Tweedmouth 1/10/61.

RENUMBERED:
60521 21/5/48.

CONDEMNED:
12/11/62.
Into Doncaster Works for cut–up 10/5/63.

522
STRAIGHT DEAL.

Doncaster 2013.

To traffic 19/6/47.

REPAIRS:
Don.10/12/47–12/2/48.**H.**
Don.11/8–29/9/49.**G.**
Don.19/12/50–18/1/51.**H/I.**
Don.25/10–22/11/51.**C/L.**
Don.11/8–18/9/52.**G.**
Don.4/5–9/6/54.**G.**
Don.9–30/6/55.**C/L.**
Don.7/2–15/3/56.**G.**
Don.26–30/11/56.**N/C.**
Don.24–26/10/57.*Weigh.*
Don.13/2–14/3/58.**G.**
Don.2/2–10/3/60.**G.**

Don.30/7–27/8/60.**C/L.**
Don.28/1–18/2/61.**C/L.**
Don.1/5–14/6/62.**G.**
Dar.3/9–21/10/64.**C/L.**

BOILERS:
3735 *Renumbered 29779 18/1/51.*
29778 (ex60514) 18/9/52.
29788 (ex60519) 9/6/54.
29854 (ex60538) 14/3/58.
29829 (ex60512) 10/3/60.
29804 (ex60523) 14/6/62.

SHEDS:
Gateshead.
York 16/8/47.
Neville Hill 18/1/48.
York 30/5/48.
Aberdeen Ferryhill 2/12/62.
St Margarets 31/12/62.
Polmadie 15/9/63.

RENUMBERED:
E522 12/2/48.
60522 29/9/49.

CONDEMNED:
19/6/65.
Sold for scrap 7/65 to Motherwell Machinery & Scrap Co.

523
SUN CASTLE.

Doncaster 2014.

To traffic 2/8/47.

REPAIRS:
Don.30/5–14/7/49.**G.**
Don.13/3–13/4/51.**H/I.**
Don.17–21/9/51.**N/C.**
Don.22/9–7/11/52.**G.**
Don.12/4–13/5/54.**G.**
Lipped chimney.
Don.31/8–22/9/54.**C/L.**
Don.16/3–7/4/55.**C/L.**
Don.13/4–1/6/56.**G.**
Don.28/5–14/6/57.**C/L.**
Don.3/2–5/3/58.**G.**
Don.6–10/3/59.**N/C.**
Don.27/10–28/11/59.**G.**
Don.14/11–21/12/61.**G.**

BOILERS:
3749 *Renumbered 29782*
13/4/51.
29779 (ex60522) 7/11/52.
29790 (ex60518) 13/5/54.
29777 (ex60521) 1/6/56.
29832 (ex60151) 5/3/58.
29804 (ex60161) 28/11/59.
29830 (ex60518) 21/12/61.

SHEDS:
Kings Cross.
Copley Hill 30/5/48.
New England 5/12/48.
Grantham 14/12/58.
New England 12/4/59.
Doncaster 10/1/60.
New England 23/9/62.

RENUMBERED:
60523 14/7/49.

CONDEMNED:
16/6/63.
Into Doncaster Works for
cut–up 28/8/63.

524
HERRINGBONE.

Doncaster 2015.

To traffic 26/9/47.

REPAIRS:
Don.22/12/48–26/1/49.**G.**
Don.9/3–6/4/49.**C/H.**
Don.6/3–11/4/51.**G.**
Don.1–8/8/51.**N/C.**
Don.1–9/10/51.**N/C.**
Don.15/12/52–16/1/53.**H/I.**
Don.9/3–6/4/54.**C/L.**
Don.6/8–14/9/54.**G.**
Don.24/5–10/7/56.**G.**
Don.8–14/8/56.**N/C.**
Don.29/5–9/7/58.**G.**
Don.13/4–21/5/60.**G.**
Don.12/9–6/10/60.**C/L.**
Don.21/9–8/11/62.**G.**
Don.13–20/11/62.**N/C.**

BOILERS:
3742.
3713 (ex60514) 26/1/49.
29781 (ex60513) 11/4/51.
29782 (ex60521) 14/9/54.
29853 (ex60535) 10/7/56.
29781 (ex60516) 9/7/58.
29791 (ex60517) 21/5/60.
29832 (ex60512) 8/11/62.

SHEDS:
York.
Neville Hill 18/1/48.
York 26/9/48.
St Margarets 2/12/62.
Aberdeen Ferryhill
31/12/62.
Polmadie 15/9/63.

RENUMBERED:
60524 26/1/49.

CONDEMNED:
15/2/65.
Sold for scrap 5/65 to
Motherwell Machinery &
Scrap Co.

WORKS CODES:– Cow – Cowlairs. Dar – Darlington. Don – Doncaster. Gat – Gateshead. Hay – Haymarket Shed. Inv – Inverurie.

REPAIR CODES:– **C/H** – Casual Heavy. **C/L** – Casual Light. **G** – General. **H** – Heavy. **H/I** – Heavy Intermediate. **L** – Light. **L/I** – Light Intermediate. **N/C** – Non–Classified.

This is the type of traffic which Thompson intended this class to work. 60517 has at least eleven coaches to haul from Newcastle to Kings Cross, and it has just observed the speed restriction for the passage of Selby swing bridge.

Not the sort of work which Thompson intended for his A2 class! 60524 ambles through Doncaster station on 23rd May 1959, with the humblest form of goods train. It still has a boiler with circular dome, but has acquired cast chimney and Automatic Warning equipment.

60521 in October 1951 at Grantham shed, ready for a return working to Newcastle. In July 1951 it was the first of the class to change to a cast type chimney. Note it has normal lamp irons, and not those adapted for electric lighting.

Going through the station to its Doncaster shed, 60523 shows its final state, which differed from the original by a change of chimney and boiler type, and by the addition of fittings for the Automatic Warning System. Note that its buffer beam lamp irons would have suited electric lighting, which it never received. The bracket for its original BTH type of speed indicator remains in place, but the equipment had long been discarded and removed.

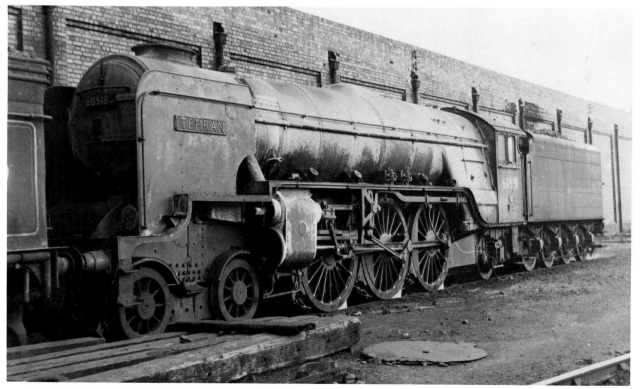

The increasing numbers of diesel locomotives put the A2/3 class out of work, and at the end of the summer traffic in 1961 and 1962, some were placed in store. On 6th October 1962 in Scarborough shed, 60516 was laid aside along with Nos. 60515, 60518 and 60522, and no more than five weeks later the only one not withdrawn was 60522, which went to Scotland.

The LNER's last day, 31st December 1947, and its newest engine is paraded in Doncaster works yard, attended by A.H. Peppercorn (for whom it was named) and 81 of those who had been primarily concerned with its design and construction. The batch of fifteen was originally ordered by his predecessor (as A2/3s) but Thompson's retirement had enabled Peppercorn to modify the design more in line with Gresley principles, on which he had been trained. No. 526 followed sufficiently closely so that it too, got LNER lettering and numbering.

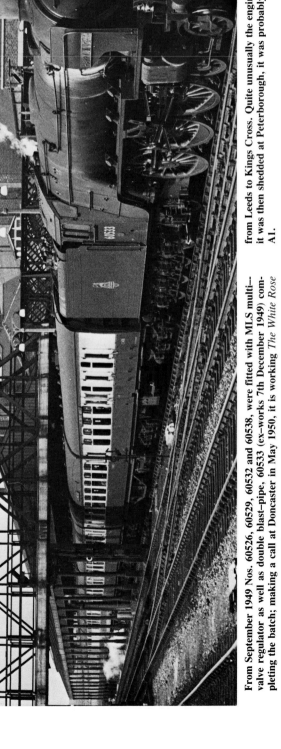

From September 1949 Nos. 60526, 60529, 60532 and 60538, were fitted with MLS multi–valve regulator as well as double blast–pipe; 60533 (ex–works 7th December 1949) completing the batch; making a call at Doncaster in May 1950, it is working *The White Rose* from Leeds to Kings Cross. Quite unusually the engine is without the train headboard. As it was then shedded at Peterborough, it was probably substituting for a failed Copley Hill A1.

PEPPERCORN A2

525
A.H.PEPPERCORN.

Doncaster 2016.

To traffic 24/12/47.

REPAIRS:
Don.13/7–25/8/49.**G.**
Don.20/6–27/7/51.**H/I.**
Cow.18–19/4/52.**N/C.**
Don.18/2–20/3/53.**G.**
Don.25/11–5/12/53.**N/C.**
Don.4/10–2/11/54.**G.**
Don.3/3–11/4/56.**G.**
Don.11–21/6/56.**N/C.**
Don.26/3–24/4/57.**C/L.**
Don.21/2–25/3/58.**G.**
Inv.7–14/5/59.**N/C.**
Don.19/8–23/9/59.**G.**
Don.28–30/9/59.**N/C.**
Don.24/4–7/6/61.**C/L.**
Don.29/9–30/11/61.**G.**
Don.29/1–27/2/63.**C/L.**

BOILERS:
9645 *Renumbered 29845
27/7/51.*
29849 (ex60141) 20/3/53.
29840 (ex60502) 2/11/54.
29834 (ex60141) 11/4/56.
29777 (ex60523) 25/3/58.
29816 (ex60534) 23/9/59.
29826 (ex60519) 30/11/61.

SHEDS:
Doncaster.
New England 12/12/48.
Aberdeen Ferryhill
28/8/49.

RENUMBERED:
60525 25/8/49.

CONDEMNED:
27/3/63.
Into St Rollox for cut–up
14/4/63.

526
SUGAR PALM.

Doncaster 2017.

To traffic 9/1/48.

REPAIRS:
Don.17–26/8/48.**L.**
Don.1–18/11/48.**L.**
Don.14/2–4/3/49.**C/L.**
Don.13/9–27/10/49.**G.**
*Multi–valve regulator and
double chimney fitted.*
Don.10/4–10/5/51.**H/I.**
Don.12/2–12/3/52.**G.**

Don.28–29/4/53.*Weigh.*
Don.1–30/7/53.**G.**
Don.27/10–4/12/54.**G.**
Don.10–21/10/56.**G.**
Don.19–22/12/56.**N/C.**
Don.7/10–7/11/58.**G.**
Don.29/12/58–16/1/59.**C/L.**
Don.7/3–14/4/61.**H/I.**
Don.25–27/4/61.**N/C.**

BOILERS:
9646 *Renumbered 29833
10/5/51.*
29812 (ex60129) 12/3/52.
29865 (ex60132) 30/7/53.
29821 (ex60158) 4/12/54.
29835 (ex60134) 7/11/58.

SHEDS:
York.
Neville Hill 18/1/48.
York 26/9/48.

RENUMBERED:
60526 26/8/48.

CONDEMNED:
12/11/62.
Into Doncaster Works for
cut–up 4/4/63.

E527
SUN CHARIOT.

Doncaster 2018.

To traffic 30/1/48.

REPAIRS:
Don.2/4–13/5/49.**G.**
Gat.16/8–8/9/50.**C/L.**
Don.30/12/50–8/2/51.**H/I.**
Cow.1–3/11/51.**N/C.**
Cow.21/11–22/12/51.**N/C.**
Don.2–31/7/52.**G.**
Don.23/10–21/11/53.**H/I.**
Don.5/5–10/6/55.**G.**
Don.10–17/8/55.**N/C.**
Don.10/5–5/6/56.**C/L.**
Don.20/8–6/9/56.**C/L.**
Don.16/4–25/5/57.**G.**
Don.4/11–18/12/58.**G.**
Don.17/3–6/4/59.**C/L.**
Don.25–30/9/59.**C/L.**
Don.8–18/3/60.**C/L.**
Don.31/10–30/11/60.**G.**
Don.4–16/12/61.**C/L.**
Cow.16/1–2/2/62.**C/L.**
Don.10/7–28/9/62.**G.**
Cow.12/3/64.*Axle test.*
Dar.16/6–21/8/64.**C/L.**

BOILERS:
9647 *Renumbered 29823
8/2/51.*

29809 (ex60513) 31/7/52.
29860 (ex60153) 10/6/55.
29778 (ex60517) 25/5/57.
29821 (ex60526) 18/12/58.
29860 (ex60535) 30/11/60.
29867 (ex60502) 28/9/62.

SHEDS:
Gateshead.
Dundee 26/6/49.
Perth 4/4/60.
Aberdeen Ferryhill
28/5/60.
Polmadie 15/9/63.

RENUMBERED:
60527 2/6/48.

CONDEMNED:
24/4/65.
Sold for scrap 6/65 to
Motherwell Machinery &
Scrap Co.

E528
TUDOR MINSTREL.

Doncaster 2019.

To traffic 21/2/48.

REPAIRS:
Don.27/4–10/6/49.**G.**
Don.11/9–4/10/50.**C/L.**
Don.26/9–31/10/51.**H/I.**
Don.11/3–15/4/53.**G.**
Don.20–23/4/53.**N/C.**
Don.17/11–21/12/54.**G.**
Cow.2–3/9/55.**N/C.**
Cow.10–12/10/55.**N/C.**
Cow.1–10/11/55.**N/C.**
Don.28/12/56–1/2/57.**G.**
Don.25/8–10/10/58.**G.**
Don.7/3–13/4/60.**G.**
Don.20/3–6/5/61.**C/L.**
Don.1/5–27/7/62.**G.**
Dar.8/2–20/5/65.**C/L.**

BOILERS:
9648 *Renumbered 29804
4/10/50.*
29858 (ex60535) 15/4/53.
29865 (ex60526) 21/12/54.
29850 (ex60124) 1/2/57.
29855 (ex60536) 10/10/58.
29788 (ex60500) 13/4/60.
29874 (ex60530) 27/7/62.

SHEDS:
Gateshead.
Dundee 26/6/49.
Perth 2/5/60.
Aberdeen Ferryhill
28/5/60.
Dundee 19/6/61.

Aberdeen Ferryhill
24/4/66.

RENUMBERED:
60528 25/6/48.

CONDEMNED:
2/6/66.
Sold for scrap 8/66 to J.
McWilliam, Shettleston.

E529
PEARL DIVER.

Doncaster 2020.

To traffic 21/2/48.

REPAIRS:
Don.18/7–16/9/49.**G.**
*Multi–valve regulator &
double chimney fitted.*
Don.22–29/9/49.**N/C.**
Don.30/7–30/8/51.**H/I.**
Don.21/1–19/2/53.**G.**
Don.28/4–28/5/54.**G.**
Don.26/10–26/11/55.**G.**
Cow.11/9–3/10/56.**C/L.**
Don.10/4–18/5/57.**G.**
Don.1–24/7/58.**C/L.**
Don.22/1–6/3/59.**G.**
Don.10/2–18/3/60.**C/L.**
Don.18/2–24/3/61.**H/I.**
Don.3/9–25/10/62.**C/L.**

BOILERS:
9649 *Renumbered 29848
30/8/51.*
29825 (ex60157) 6/3/59.

SHEDS:
Haymarket.
St Margarets 16/10/61.

RENUMBERED:
60529 16/9/49.

CONDEMNED:
29/12/62.
Sold for scrap 6/64 to
G.H.Campbell, Airdrie.

E530
SAYAJIRAO.

Doncaster 2021.

To traffic 4/3/48.

REPAIRS:
Don.22/10–17/11/48.**L.**
Don.26–28/4/49.**N/C.**
Don.30–31/5/49.*Weigh.*
Don.7/11–9/12/49.**G.**
Don.7/5–8/6/51.**H/I.**

WORKS CODES:– Cow – Cowlairs. Dar – Darlington. Don – Doncaster. Gat – Gateshead. Hay – Haymarket Shed. Inv – Inverurie.

REPAIR CODES:– **C/H** – Casual Heavy. **C/L** – Casual Light. **G** – General. **H** – Heavy. **H/I** – Heavy Intermediate. **L** – Light. **L/I** – Light Intermediate. **N/C** – Non–Classified.

The next five, Nos. 527 to 531 and new to traffic from 30th November to 12th March 1948, had BRITISH RAILWAYS as tender lettering, and an E prefix to the number. Only 527 had the prefix in front of the figures, and here it is at Chaloner Whin junction working the up *Flying Scotsman* from Newcastle to Grantham, in February 1948.

On Nos. 528 to 531 the E prefix – indicating which region was responsible for maintenance – was placed *above* the figures, both on buffer beam and on cab side. 530 with *KINGS X* shed allocation on its buffer beam is backing out of that station.

Cow.16–18/6/52.**N/C.**
Don.31/3–8/5/53.**G.**
Don.15/1–26/2/54.**G.**
Don.25/7–22/9/55.**G.**
Don.5/1–9/2/57.**G.**
Don.30/7–19/9/58.**G.**
Don.24/1–11/2/59.**C/L.**
Don.14–19/3/59.**N/C.**
Don.7/6–21/7/60.**G.**
Don.6/4–17/5/62.**G.**
Cow.16/3/64.*Axle test.*
Dar.1/9–8/10/64.**C/L.**

BOILERS:
9650 *Renumbered* 29839
8/6/51.
29816 (ex60121) 8/5/53.
29868 (ex60537) 26/2/54.
29814 (ex60132) 22/9/55.
29807 (ex60501) 9/2/57.
29853 (ex60524) 19/9/58.
29874 (ex60162) 21/7/60.
29879 (ex60539) 17/5/62.

SHEDS:
Kings Cross.
New England 12/12/48.
Haymarket 9/1/50.
St Margarets 16/10/61.
Polmadie 15/9/63.
Dundee 31/7/64.

RENUMBERED:
60530 17/11/48.

CONDEMNED:
19/11/66.
Sold for scrap 3/67 to
Motherwell Machinery &
Scrap Co.

E531
BAHRAM.

Doncaster 2022.

To traffic 12/3/48.

REPAIRS:
Don.11/5–23/6/49.**G.**
Don.4/12/50–12/1/51.**H/I.**
Inv.25–28/3/52.**N/C.**
Don.23/9–23/10/52.**G.**
Don.1/2–9/3/54.**G.**
Don.10/12/54–7/1/55.**C/L.**
Don.14/2–3/3/55.**C/L.**
Don.11/10–14/11/55.**G.**
Don.7–24/2/56.**C/L.**
Don.7/8–5/9/57.**G.**
Don.23/2–2/4/59.**G.**
Don.14–17/4/59.**N/C.**
Don.24/11–30/12/60.**G.**
Don.29/10/62 – *Not
repaired.*

BOILERS:
9651 *Renumbered* 29822
12/1/51.
29832 (ex60116) 23/10/52.
29836 (ex60114) 9/3/54.
29868 (ex60530) 14/11/55.

29860 (ex60527) 5/9/57.
29852 (ex60520) 2/4/59.
29821 (ex60527) 30/12/60.

SHEDS:
Gateshead.
Aberdeen Ferryhill 7/8/49.
York 2/12/62.

RENUMBERED:
60531 25/11/48.

CONDEMNED:
10/12/62.
Cut–up instead of being
repaired.

60532
BLUE PETER.

Doncaster 2023.

To traffic 25/3/48.

REPAIRS:
Don.11/8–28/9/49.**G.**
*Multi–valve regulator &
double chimney fitted.*
Don.28/2–4/4/51.**G.**
Don.12–17/4/51.**N/C.**
Don.14/8–6/9/51.**C/L.** *After
derailment.*
Don.11/6–23/7/52.**H/I.**
Cow.28–29/1/53.**N/C.**
Don.19/11–19/12/53.**G.**
Don.16/3–22/4/55.**G.**
Don.19–26/7/55.**C/L.**
Don.8–15/2/56.**C/L.**
Don.21/3–4/4/56.**C/L.**
Don.28/1–1/3/57.**G.**
Don.24/7–28/8/58.**H/I.**
Don.29/12/59–4/2/60.**H/I.**
Don.10/8–24/9/60.**C/L.**
Don.14/12/60–5/1/61.**C/L.**
Don.10/3–15/4/61.**C/L.**
Cow.1–14/12/61.**C/L.**
Don.6/6–26/7/62.**G.**
Inv.14–15/4/64.**N/C.**
Dar.4/2–18/5/65.**L/I.**

BOILERS:
9652.
29830 (ex60151) 4/4/51.
29801 (ex60537) 1/3/57.
29871 (ex60535) 26/7/62.

SHEDS:
York.
Haymarket 27/11/49.
Aberdeen Ferryhill 7/1/51.
Dundee 19/6/61.
Aberdeen Ferryhill
4/12/66.

WITHDRAWN:
31/12/66. Sold for
preservation 21/8/68.

60533
HAPPY KNIGHT.

Doncaster 2024.

To traffic 9/4/48.

REPAIRS:
Don.31/10–7/12/49.**G.**
*Multi–valve regulator &
double chimney fitted.*
Don.23–25/5/50.**C/L.**
Don.12–14/6/50.**C/L.**
Don.19–26/7/50.**C/L.**
Don.28/9–27/10/50.**C/L.**
Don.16/10–19/11/51.**G.**
Don.13/4–9/5/53.**G.**
Don.6–8/10/53.**N/C.**
Don.25/11–31/12/54.**G.**
Don.22/3–4/5/56.**G.**
Don.14–15/5/56.**N/C.**
Don.21/1/57.*Weigh.*
Don.22/2–7/3/57.**C/L.**
Don.11/1–14/2/58.**G.**
Don.18/7–11/8/58.**C/L.**
Don.19–22/8/58.**N/C.**
Don.1/10–4/11/59.**G.**
Don.11–22/9/61.**N/C.**
Don.4–19/10/61.**N/C.**
Don.10/11/61.*Weigh.*
Don.8/6–10/8/62.**G.**

BOILERS:
9653 *Renumbered* 29810
19/11/51.
29857 (ex60117) 9/5/53.
29815 (ex60121) 31/12/54.
29822 (ex60140) 4/5/56.
29806 (ex60158) 14/2/58.
29862 (ex60143) 4/11/59.
29848 (ex60538) 10/8/62.

SHEDS:
New England.
Copley Hill 29/5/48.
New England 19/12/48.
Copley Hill 12/3/50.
New England 30/4/50.
Annesley 2/7/50.
New England 9/7/50.
Grantham 20/6/54.
New England 16/9/56.
Grantham 15/9/57.
Kings Cross 8/6/58.
Grantham 14/12/58.
New England 14/6/59.
Doncaster 10/1/60.
New England 23/9/62.

CONDEMNED:
15/6/63.
Into Doncaster Works
2/9/63 for cut–up.

60534
IRISH ELEGANCE.

Doncaster 2025.

To traffic 23/4/48.

REPAIRS:
Don.11–26/11/48.**L.**
Don.24/3–6/4/49.**C/L.**

Don.16/1–24/3/50.**G.**
Don.24/9–24/10/51.**H/I.**
Don.22/2–25/3/53.**G.**
Don.3/5–9/6/54.**H/I.**
Don.15–29/3/55.**C/L.**
Hay.16/5–12/7/55.**C/L.**
Don.31/8–27/9/55.**C/L.**
Don.16/11–7/12/55.**C/L.**
Don.7/2–16/3/56.**C/L.**
Don.29/9–26/10/57.**G.**
Don.22/10–6/11/58.**N/C.**
Don.28/4–3/6/59.**G.**
Don.14/1–21/2/61.**G.**

BOILERS:
9654 *Renumbered* 29853
24/10/51.
29845 (ex60525) 25/3/53.
29829 (ex60116) 16/3/56.
29816 (ex60160) 26/10/57.
29780 (ex60535) 3/6/59.
29852 (ex60531) 21/2/61.

SHEDS:
York.
Haymarket 27/11/49.
St Margarets 13/11/61.

CONDEMNED:
29/12/62.
Sold for scrap 6/64 to
G.H.Campbell, Airdrie.

60535
HORNETS BEAUTY.

Doncaster 2026.

To traffic 5/5/48.

REPAIRS:
Don.15–28/9/48.**L.** *After
collision.*
Don.5–14/4/49.**C/L.**
Don.4–19/5/50.**G.**
Don.30/10–30/11/51.**H/I.**
Cow.22–24/5/52.**N/C.**
Don.4/3–2/4/53.**G.**
Don.24/5–2/7/54.**H/I.**
Don.1–14/3/55.**C/L.**
Don.29/12/55–2/2/56.**G.**
Don.25/11–20/12/57.**G.**
Don.19/3–28/4/59.**G.**
Don.16/8–29/9/60.**G.**
Don.27/3–5/5/62.**G.**

BOILERS:
9655 *Renumbered* 29858
30/11/51.
29853 (ex60534) 2/4/53.
29846 (ex60136) 2/2/56.
29780 (ex60512) 20/12/57.
29860 (ex60531) 28/4/59.
29871 (ex60130) 29/9/60.
29847 (ex60143) 5/5/62.

SHEDS:
York.
Haymarket 27/11/49.
St Margarets 16/10/61.
Polmadie 15/9/63.

WORKS CODES:– Cow – Cowlairs. Dar – Darlington. Don – Doncaster. Gat – Gateshead. Hay – Haymarket Shed. Inv – Inverurie.

REPAIR CODES:– **C/H** – Casual Heavy. **C/L** – Casual Light. **G** – General. **H** – Heavy. **H/I** – Heavy Intermediate. **L** – Light. **L/I** – Light Intermediate. **N/C** – Non–Classified.

CONDEMNED:
19/6/65.
Sold for scrap 7/65 to
Motherwell Machinery &
Scrap Co.

60536
TRIMBUSH.

Doncaster 2027.

To traffic 14/5/48.

REPAIRS:
Don.14/6–21/7/50.**G.**
Don.25/7/50.**N/C.**
Don.31/7–4/8/50.**N/C.**
Don.8/10–7/11/51.**H/I.**
Don.5/11–12/12/52.**H/I.**
Don.4–10/3/53.**N/C.**
Don.13–25/8/53.**N/C.**
Don.2/6–16/7/54.**G.**
Don.26–30/7/54.**N/C.**
Don.7–16/3/55.**C/L.**
Don.29/4–9/5/55.**N/C.**
Cow.12–17/9/55.**N/C.**
Don.10/2–16/3/56.**G.**
Don.3–15/10/56.**C/L.**
Don.30/4–18/5/57.**C/L.**
Don.27/11–28/12/57.**G.**
Don.15/7–19/8/59.**G.**
Don.23/3–29/4/61.**G.**
Don.17/12/62 – *Not
repaired.*

BOILERS:
9656 *Renumbered 29855
7/11/51.*
29875 (ex60143) 28/12/57.
29833 (ex60138) 19/8/59.
29781 (ex60524) 29/4/61.

SHEDS:
Copley Hill.
New England 26/12/48.
Haymarket 20/11/49.
St Margarets 13/11/61.
Haymarket 14/5/62.

St Margarets 8/10/62.
York 2/12/62.

CONDEMNED:
17/12/62.
Cut–up Doncaster Works.

60537
BACHELORS BUTTON.

Doncaster 2028.

To traffic 11/6/48.

REPAIRS:
Don.6–14/7/48.**L.**
Don.26/7–30/8/50.**G.**
Don.20/9–25/10/51.**C/L.**
Don.19/6–31/7/52.**H/I.**
Don.16/12/53–15/1/54.**G.**
Don.24/2–25/3/55.**G.**
Don.28/9–14/11/56.**G.**
Don.24/3–1/5/58.**G.**
Don.3–18/10/58.**C/L.**
Don.16/9–21/10/59.**G.**
A.W.S. fitted.
Don.28/8–13/10/61.**G.**

BOILERS:
9657 *Renumbered 29868
31/7/52.*
29866 (ex60127) 15/1/54.
29801 (ex60119) 25/3/55.
29837 (ex60145) 14/11/56.
29790 (ex60500) 1/5/58.
29789 (ex60516) 21/10/59.
29833 (ex60536) 13/10/61.

SHEDS:
Copley Hill.
New England 2/1/49.
Aberdeen Ferryhill 1/7/49.
Haymarket 7/1/51.
St Margarets 13/11/61.

CONDEMNED:
29/12/62.

Sold for scrap 6/64 to
Hendersons, Airdrie.

60538
VELOCITY.

Doncaster 2029.

To traffic 18/6/48.

REPAIRS:
Don.26/9–28/10/49.**G.**
*Multi–valve regulator &
double chimney fitted.*
Don.21–26/9/50.*Special
Exam.*
Don.12/3–11/4/51.**G.**
Don.3–16/1/52.**C/L.** *After
derailment.*
Don.16/7–20/8/52.**H/I.**
Gat.4–7/5/53.**C/L.**
Don.5/11–4/12/53.**G.**
Don.16/2–24/3/55.**G.**
Don.30/4–6/6/56.**G.**
Don.29/7–7/8/57.**C/L.**
Don.13/1–15/2/58.**G.**
Don.17–25/9/58.**N/C.**
Don.10/6–23/7/59.**G.**
Don.3/10–9/11/61.**G.**

BOILERS:
9658 *Renumbered 29806
26/9/50.*
29854 (ex60144) 4/12/53.
29822 (ex60533) 15/2/58.
29848 (ex60529) 23/7/59.
29822 (ex60150) 9/11/61.

SHEDS:
Gateshead.
Heaton 22/5/60.
Tweedmouth 1/10/61.

CONDEMNED:
12/11/62.
Into Doncaster Works for
cut–up 13/5/63.

60539
BRONZINO.

Doncaster 2030.

To traffic 27/8/48 with
Kylchap double blastpipe
& chimney.

REPAIRS:
Don.1–22/4/49.**C/L.**
Modified for trials.
Don.23/5/49.*Weigh.*
Dar.13/6/49.*Weigh.*
Don.6/2–14/4/50.**G.**
Dar.5/9/50.*Weigh.*
Don.8–31/1/51.**H/I.**
Don.14/5–6/6/52.**C/L.**
Don.3/12/52–2/1/53.**G.**
Don.9/3–7/4/54.**G.**
Don.17/5–9/6/55.**C/L.**
Don.3/10–7/11/55.**G.**
Don.18/7–22/8/57.**G.**
Don.24/3–1/5/59.**G.**
Don.12/6–1/7/59.**C/L.**
Don.1/12/60–5/1/61.**G.**

BOILERS:
9660 *Renumbered 29825
31/1/51.*
29803 (ex60135) 2/1/53.
29844 (ex60159) 7/4/54.
29824 (ex60133) 7/11/55.
29830 (ex60532) 22/8/57.
29879 (ex60117) 1/5/59.
29810 (ex60148) 5/1/61.

SHEDS:
Heaton.
Tweedmouth 1/10/61.

CONDEMNED:
12/11/62.
Into Doncaster Works for
cut–up 19/4/63.

BLUE PETER on a King's Cross – Leeds and Bradford express, about to enter Gas Works tunnel, only 24 chains from Kings Cross station. By the time *BLUE PETER* had entered traffic, on 25th March 1948, five figure numbering has ousted the prefix, and in BR service it always carried 60532.

The five with double chimney were widely spread, and 60538 represented the class at Gateshead shed. Here it is near Longniddry, working the 10.30am ex–Edinburgh, on which the first two vehicles are Royal Mail vans. When the five changed to double blast–pipe, they first had to make do with a sheet metal chimney, though with a beading round the rim.

The unsightly sheet metal chimney was duly replaced on all five by this cast iron version, to the distinct advantage of its appearance, but the external operating rod for the multi–valve regulator always looked to be an untidy afterthought. This is 60533 from its February 1958 shopping, by then with electric lighting removed.

The last of the batch, 60539 had Kylchap double blast–pipe from new, with a sheet metal chimney, but it was never fitted with multi–valve regulator. All fifteen were equipped with electric lighting, for which the generator was a steam turbine driven unit, made by J. Stone and mounted inside the right hand smoke deflector.

60534 in July 1958, on the turntable at Haymarket, its home shed. The front vacuum hosepipe has been connected to the mechanism for turning the table. Note that by this time the electric lighting equipment has been removed completely.

Haymarket's 60535, at Perth on 2nd June 1951, about to return to Edinburgh. Ten out of the fifteen did most of their work from sheds in Scotland. The electric generator is clear to see in this view, along with the dual–purpose lamp irons which allowed the use of oil lamps.

60530 at Kings Cross in May 1962, running–in after general repair before return to its home shed of St. Margarets in Edinburgh. It had lost electric lighting but in February 1959 Automatic Warning System had been fitted, and in July 1960 it had been provided with Smith–Stone speed indicator.

60536 *TRIMBUSH* was one of seven in this class which, between May 1958 and April 1961 were fitted with a boiler originally built for Thompson's A2/3 class. They had a circular dome, further forward than the normal steam collector used by the A2 class. 60536 is at Carlisle Canal shed on 25th March 1962, having worked over the Waverley route.

60532 provides illustration of what a N/C (non–classified) repair could entail. It was in Doncaster works from 28th February to 4th April 1951 for general repair, but would not be sent back to its Aberdeen shed until the works were satisfied as to its condition. After Doncaster shed had given it some jobs, it was called back into the works on 12th April; it is seen here on 15th when the driving wheels have been taken out for the bearings to be adjusted.

When 60532 was withdrawn from stock on 31st December 1966, it was the last one of the Peppercorn A2 class and his A1 class had been extinct from the previous June. Very fortunately 60532 was laid aside because interest had been expressed in buying it for preservation instead of for scrapping. The sale was duly completed on 21st August 1968, for the engine to be kept in running condition, and not restored simply as a museum exhibit somewhere. In November 1970 it has been prepared to take part in an Open Day at Doncaster Works which was linked with the BBC's *Blue Peter* children's programme, with its presenters in attendance. Even they were amazed when the visitors totalled around the 50,000 mark! Purists should note that *BLUE PETER* never was LNER 532 and whilst it did originally have apple–green painting, that was never applied to its cylinder casings when it was in normal use.

Until April 1950, only the first engine had been named, but pressure on British Railways persuaded them to incur the cost of plates for the others. All the names chosen were in line with LNER tradition, but unusual for the variety in a single class. Thirteen took names of racehorses; eighteen had been used by NBR engines and one of its Clyde paddle steamers; six got names of birds – four of which had once been borne by A4s; one

extended those used on the B17s; four had names of the constituent companies of the LNER, and the other six honoured North Eastern and Great Northern locomotive superintendents. *H.A. IVATT* on 60123 was one of the latter, all six of which involved official naming ceremonies. Note that naming usually preceded the change of chimney.

In the second batch built by Doncaster just one, No. 60158 to traffic on 17th November 1949, had this cast iron chimney from new. This so improved the appearance that, from

December 1950, the cost of fitting all the others was regarded as justified, and was duly implemented.

PEPPERCORN A1

60114
W.P.ALLEN from 26/10/48.

Doncaster 2031.

To traffic 6/8/48.

REPAIRS:
Don.24–26/8/48.**N/C.**
Don.9–13/10/48.**N/C.**
Don.18–26/10/48.**N/C.**
Nameplates fitted.
Don.4–28/4/49.**C/L.**
Don.10/10–16/11/49.**G.**
Don.8/3/50.*Weigh.*
Don.17–24/3/50.**C/L.**
Don.21/2–22/3/51.**H/I.**
Don.14/7–15/8/52.**G.**
Don.6–20/1/53.**C/L.**
Don.23/7/53.*Weigh.*
Don.20/1–25/2/54.**G.**
Don.24/8/54.*Weigh.*
Don.14/6–20/7/55.**G.**
Don.13–22/12/55.**C/L.**
Don.6/3–5/4/57.**G.**
Don.22/8/58.*Weigh.*
Don.27/10–5/12/58.**G.**
Don.19/6–25/7/59.**C/L.**
Don.19/5–13/7/60.**G.**
Don.17/7–19/8/62.**G.**
Don.24–27/9/62.**N/C.**
Don.13/5–12/6/63.**C/L.**

BOILERS:
9659 *renumbered 29829 22/3/51.*
29836 (ex60156) 15/8/52.
29806 (ex60538) 25/2/54.
29874 (ex60148) 20/7/55.
29873 (ex60144) 5/4/57.
29814 (ex60125) 5/12/58.
29831 (ex60115) 13/7/60.
29809 (ex60123) 19/8/62.

SHEDS:
Kings Cross.
Copley Hill 4/6/50.
Grantham 15/2/53.
Doncaster 22/9/57.

CONDEMNED:
26/12/64.
Sold for scrap 2/65 to
Hughes Bolckow, Blyth.

60115
MEG MERRILIES from 6/50.

Doncaster 2032.

To traffic 3/9/48.

REPAIRS:
Don.19/4–2/6/50.**G.**

Don.25/4–29/5/51.**G.**
Don.15/8–19/9/52.**G.**
Don.5/1–6/2/54.**G.**
Don.30/3–6/5/55.**G.**
Don.9/8–21/9/56.**G.**
Don.2/7/57.*Weigh.*
Don.26–3–6/5/58.**G.**
Don.9/12/59–15/1/60.**G.**
Don.18–20/7/60.**N/C.**
Don.16/9–15/10/60.**C/L.**
Don.9–26/5/62.**N/C.**

BOILERS:
9661 *renumbered 29837 29/5/51.*
29829 (ex60114) 19/9/52.
29872 (ex60505) 6/2/54.
29785 (ex60149) 21/9/56.
29831 (ex60131) 6/5/58.
29856 (ex60149) 15/1/60.

SHEDS:
Gateshead.
Copley Hill 20/11/60.

CONDEMNED:
12/11/62.
Into Doncaster for cut–up
24/5/63.

60116
HAL O' THE WYND from 5/51.

Doncaster 2033.

To traffic 8/10/48.

REPAIRS:
Don.10/1–22/3/50.**G.**
Dar.17/10/50.*Weigh.*
Don.4/4–1/5/51.**H/I.**
Don.24/7–22/8/52.**G.**
Don.26/1–20/2/53.**C/L.**
Don.28/1–9/3/54.**G.**
Don.16/7–10/8/54.**C/L.**
Gat.15–20/10/54.**C/L.**
Smokebox tube plate welded.
Don.15/7–24/8/55.**G.**
Don.1–9/11/56.**N/C.**
Don.21/1–22/2/57.**G.**
Don.28/10–14/11/57.**C/L.**
Don.6/8–19/9/58.**G.**
Don.29/9–2/10/58.**N/C.**
Don.4/12/59–12/1/60.**G.**
Don.8–17/8/60.**C/L.**
Don.25/11–16/12/60.**N/C.**
Don.5–23/2/62.**C/L.**
Don.26/4–2/6/62.**G.**

BOILERS:
9662 *renumbered 29832 1/5/51.*
29818 (ex60148) 22/8/52.
29829 (ex60115) 9/3/54.

29861 (ex60150) 24/8/55.
29810 (ex60127) 22/2/57.
29864 (ex60127) 19/9/58.
29803 (ex60147) 12/1/60.
29786 (ex60139) 2/6/62.

SHEDS:
Heaton.
Tweedmouth 9/9/62.
Gateshead 18/10/64.

CONDEMNED:
14/6/65.
Sold for scrap 7/65 to
Hughes Bolckow, Blyth.

60117
BOIS ROUSSEL from 7/50.

Doncaster 2034.

To traffic 22/10/48.

REPAIRS:
Don.15–17/11/48.**N/C.**
Don.16/5–6/7/50.**G.**
Don.30/10–3/11/50.**C/L.**
Don.15/10–20/11/51.**H/I.**
Don.5–11/2/53.**N/C.**
A.T.C. fitted.
Don.7/4–6/5/53.**G.**
Don.9–24/11/53.**C/L.**
Don.11/10/54.*Weigh.*
Don.20/12/54–22/1/55.**G.**
Don.8–23/12/55.**C/L.**
Don.19/4–11/5/56.**C/L.**
Don.17/10–21/11/56.**G.**
Don.20–27/9/57.**N/C.**
Don.15/3–2/4/58.**C/H.**
Don.25/11/58–7/1/59.**G.**
Don.14/10–16/11/60.**G.**
Don.16/4–22/5/63.**C/L.**

BOILERS:
9663 *renumbered 29857 20/11/51.*
29839 (ex60530) 6/5/53.
29847 (ex60130) 22/1/55.
29879 (ex60148) 21/11/56.
29827 (ex60143) 7/1/59.
29849 (ex60151) 16/11/60.

SHEDS:
Grantham.
Copley Hill 4/6/50.
Grantham 18/5/52.
Copley Hill 15/2/53.
Ardsley 6/9/64.
Gateshead 6/12/64.
Ardsley 3/1/65.

CONDEMNED:
21/6/65.
Sold for scrap 8/65 to
Clayton & Davie,
Dunston.

60118
ARCHIBALD STURROCK from 7/50.

Doncaster 2035.

To traffic 12/11/48.

REPAIRS:
Don.6–8/12/48.**L.**
Don.3/4–12/5/50.**G.**
Don.10–13/7/50.**N/C.**
Don.24–28/9/50.**C/L.**
Don.17/12/51–22/1/52.**H/I.**
Don.18/2/52.*Weigh.*
Don.4–10/2/53.**N/C.**
A.T.C. fitted.
Don.6–31/7/53.**G.**
Don.16–20/9/53.**N/C.** *For Doncaster Works Centenary Exhibition.*
Don.6/4–14/5/55.**G.**
Don.12/9/55.*Weigh.*
Don.13/3–12/4/57.**G.**
Don.14–30/10/57.**C/L.**
Don.5/1–17/2/59.**G.**
Don.6–11/6/59.**N/C.**
Don.15–21/10/59.**N/C.**
Don.5–19/12/59.**C/L.**
Don.17/3–21/4/60.**C/L.**
Don.16/2–29/3/61.**G.**
Don.29/5–12/7/62.**C/L.**
Don.11/3–5/4/63.**C/L.**
Dar.6/8–19/9/64.**C/L.**
Fractured cylinder.

BOILERS:
9664 *renumbered 29864 22/1/52.*
29813 (ex60147) 31/7/53.
29878 (New) 14/5/55.
29865 (ex60152) 17/2/59.
29880 (New) 29/3/61.

SHEDS:
Copley Hill.
Ardsley 4/11/62.
Neville Hill 28/7/63.

CONDEMNED:
4/10/65.
Sold for scrap 11/65 to
T.W.Ward, Beighton.

60119
PATRICK STIRLING from 7/50.

Doncaster 2036.

To traffic 26/11/48.

REPAIRS:
Don.28–31/12/48.**L.**
Don.5–9/1/50.**C/L.**

WORKS CODES:– Cow – Cowlairs. Dar – Darlington. Don – Doncaster. Gat – Gateshead. Hay – Haymarket Shed. Inv – Inverurie.

REPAIR CODES:– **C/H** – Casual Heavy. **C/L** – Casual Light. **G** – General. **H** – Heavy. **H/I** – Heavy Intermediate. **L** – Light. **L/I** – Light Intermediate. **N/C** – Non–Classified.

60136 illustrates the original appearance of this class, ordered in LNER days but only beginning to appear and go into traffic from August 1948. They had boiler with steam collector ('banjo dome') centred on the third cleading band, were fitted for electric lighting, had sheet metal chimney with beaded edge, and apart from one special case, were not named. They had double blastpipe and chimney to suit.

60118, always a Leeds engine, at Grantham station in 1953. Starting in December 1950, all had the sheet metal chimney replaced by a cast type; similar to that tried initially on 60158 it made for a distinctly improved appearance.

The standard boiler had the 'banjo' steam collector, centred above the middle coupled wheels, but from May 1955 no less than sixteen, at some time, carried a A2/3 Thompson boiler. These had a circular dome, further forward and on the front barrel ring, but of the A1s only 60153 was fitted with a matching cover.

Apart from 60153 (and possibly 60149) subsequent change to the A2/3 boiler carried on the A1s could only be discerned by the forward position of the dome, because the 'banjo' cover was used for them, as here on 60139, in August 1958. It is leaving Kings Cross shed for the station to take up a working.

Doncaster's first batch, Nos. 60114 to 60129, were equipped with Flaman speed recorder, driven from the right hand coupling pin but only four of the Darlington-built engines, Nos. 60130, 60133, 60134, and 60136 got them. During 1950–1951 those recorders were removed but some engines kept the supporting bracket for quite a while. Through the 1950s inspectors reporting on various accidents frequently drew attention to drivers misjudging speed, and the need for them to be given reasonably accurate knowledge of it. So between March 1960 and May 1963 all the 49 A1 Pacifics were fitted with Smith–Stone speed indicator. It was driven off the left hand rear coupling pin and did not require any support bracket. The box by the cab footsteps on 60134 contained the batteries for electrical operation of the Automatic Warning System.

The war had stopped development of the Hudd type Automatic Train Control and trials were resumed in October 1949. 60149 was fitted with it for working over the track equipment installed from King's Cross as far as Huntingdon – visible evidence is the large plate to prevent the front coupling swinging and causing damage to the signal receiving unit. The train is *The White Rose*, at Ganwick, on 8th September 1951.

60119 Continued

Don.25/4–7/6/50.**G.**
Don.10–13/7/50.**N/C.**
Don.23–26/10/50.**C/L.**
Don.21/1–19/2/52.**G.**
Don.9–15/2/53.**N/C.**
A.T.C. fitted.
Don.24/8–1/10/53.**G.**
Don.23/8/54.*Weigh.*
Don.2/2–9/3/55.**G.**
Don.29/7–14/8/55.**C/L.**
Don.13/9/55.*Weigh.*
Don.25/1–3/2/56.**C/L.**
Don.1–7/9/56.**N/C.**
Don.18/10–24/11/56.**G.**
Don.15–31/8/57.**C/L.**
Don.30/1–27/2/58.**H/I.**
Don.30/1–13/2/59.**C/L.**
Don.9–12/3/59**N/C.**
Don.20/11–24/12/59.**G.**
Don.23/4–1/6/60.**C/H.**
Don.25–29/7/60.**N/C.**
Don.4–11/11/60.**N/C.**
Don.26/5–7/6/61.**N/C.**
Don.1–25/8/61.**C/L.**
Don.24/1–24/2/62.**G.**

BOILERS:
9665.
29870 (New) 19/2/52.
29801 (ex60151) 1/10/53.
29859 (ex60146) 9/3/55.
29843 (ex60147) 24/11/56.
29806 (ex60533) 24/12/59.
29855 (ex60157) 24/2/62.

SHEDS:
Copley Hill.
Grantham 18/12/55.
Kings Cross 15/9/57.
Doncaster 3/8/58.

CONDEMNED:
31/5/64.
Sold for scrap 8/64 to Cox & Danks, Wadsley Bridge.

60120
KITTIWAKE *from 5/50.*

Doncaster 2037.

To traffic 10/12/48.

REPAIRS:
Don.23/1–31/3/50.**G.**
Don.9/8/50.*Weigh.*
Don.2–19/10/50.**C/L.**
Don.27/8–4/10/51.**H/I.**
Don.3–25/7/52.**C/L.**
Don.21–30/1/53.**N/C.**
A.T.C. fitted.
Don.26/5–9/7/53.**G.**
Don.18/3–23/4/55.**G.**
Don.3/5/55.**N/C.**
Don.13–28/4/56.**N/C.**
Don.11–17/5/56.**N/C.**
Don.31/8–21/9/56.**N/C.**
Don.14/2–25/5/57.**H/I.**
Don.17/7/57.*Weigh.*
Don.24/1–3/2/58.**N/C.**
Don.11–26/9/58.**N/C.**

Don.1/4–6/5/59.**G.**
Don.11/2–2/3/60.**C/L.**
Don.14/5–17/6/60.**C/L.**
Don.18/7–24/8/61.**G.**

BOILERS:
9666 *renumbered 29811 4/10/51.*
29857 (ex60533) 23/4/55.
29859 (ex60130) 6/5/59.
29881 (New) 24/8/61.

SHEDS:
Kings Cross.
Copley Hill 4/6/50.
York 8/9/63.

CONDEMNED:
20/1/64.
Into Darlington Works for cut–up 28/1/64.

60121
SILURIAN *from 5/50.*

Doncaster 2038.

To traffic 22/12/48.

REPAIRS:
Don.21/6–8/7/49.**C/L.**
Don.11/4–19/5/50.**G.**
Don.23–26/5/50.**N/C.**
Don.4–11/7/51.**N/C.**
Don.19/11–20/12/51.**G.**
Don.18/11/52.*Weigh.*
Don.25/3–29/4/53.**G.**
Don.10/11–14/12/54.**G.**
Don.21–24/12/54.**N/C.**
Don.21/2–3/4/57.**G.**
Don.28–30/5/57.**N/C.**
Don.14–22/10/58.**N/C.**
Don.16/12/58.*Weigh.*
Don.12/12/59–22/1/60.**G.**
Don.8–12/7/60.**N/C.**
Don.8–20/4/61.**C/L.**
Don.22/10–2/11/62.**N/C.**
Don.20/3–15/5/63.**G.**
Don.22–27/5/63.**N/C.**
Don.6–14/6/63.**N/C.**
Don.1–25/7/63.**C/L.**

BOILERS:
9667.
29816 (ex60146) 20/12/51.
29815 (ex60136) 29/4/53.
29800 (ex60129) 14/12/54.
29839 (ex60139) 3/4/57.
29864 (ex60116) 22/1/60.
29863 (ex60124) 15/5/63.

SHED:
York.

CONDEMNED:
4/10/65.
Sold for scrap 11/65 to T.W.Ward, Killamarsh.

60122
CURLEW *from 7/50.*

Doncaster 2039.

To traffic 24/12/48.

REPAIRS:
Don.4–10/1/49.**N/C.**
Don.18–21/1/49.**N/C.**
Don.27/3–5/5/50.**G.**
Don.7/5–13/6/51.**G.**
Don.16–25/10/51.**N/C.**
Don.26/8–2/10/52.**G.**
Don.4–14/11/52.**C/L.**
Don.22/2–24/3/54.**G.**
Don.19–27/8/54.**N/C.**
Don.17–25/11/54.**N/C.**
Don.22/9–18/10/55.**C/L.**
Don.24/1–2/3/56.**G.**
Don.23/7–24/8/57.**G.**
Don.2–18/12/57.**C/L.**
Don.14–23/5/58.**N/C.**
Don.22–29/4/59.**C/L.**
Don.16/9–23/10/59.**G.**
Don.16–25/11/60.**N/C.**
Don.14/8–22/9/61.**G.**
Don.17–24/10/62.**C/L.**
Don.11/12/62.*Not repaired.*

BOILERS:
9668 *renumbered 29840 13/6/51.*
29823 (ex60527) 2/10/52.
29818 (ex60116) 24/3/54.
29804 (ex60162) 2/3/56.
29844 (ex60136) 24/8/57.
29813 (ex60150) 23/10/59.
29815 (ex60156) 22/9/61.

SHEDS:
Kings Cross.
Gateshead 9/9/51.
Copley Hill 18/10/53.
Grantham 28/8/55.
Kings Cross 15/9/57.
Doncaster 5/4/59.

CONDEMNED:
17/12/62.
Cut–up Doncaster.

60123
H.A.IVATT *from 7/50.*

Doncaster 2040.

To traffic 10/2/49.

REPAIRS:
Don.14–16/2/49.**N/C.**
Don.18–23/2/49.**N/C.**
Don.7/11–9/12/49.**C/L.**
Don.30/12/49–13/1/50.**C/L.**
Don.10–13/7/50.**N/C.**
Don.16–20/10/50.**C/L.**
Don.16/4–11/5/51.**H/I.**
Don.24/3–1/4/52.**N/C.**
Don.14/11–17/12/52.**G.**
Don.17–22/2/53.**N/C.**
Don.6/8–25/9/54.**G.**
Don.9/11/54.*Weigh.*
Don.27/2–11/4/56.**G.**
Don.17/4/56.*Weigh.*

Don.19/12/57–22/1/58.**G.**
Don.20–24/3/58.**N/C.**
Don.20–26/9/58.**N/C.**
Don.24/4–9/5/59.**N/C.**
Don.25/1–1/3/60.**C/L.**
Don.12/4–25/5/62.**G.**
Don.24/9/62 – *Not repaired.*

BOILERS:
9669 *Renumbered 29834 11/5/51.*
29852 (ex60126) 17/12/52.
29808 (ex60126) 25/9/54.
29846 (ex60535) 22/1/58.
29809 (ex60155) 1/3/60.
29866 (ex60127) 25/5/62.

SHEDS:
Doncaster.
Grantham 19/3/50.
Copley Hill 4/6/50.
Ardsley 9/9/51.
Copley Hill 15/9/57.
Ardsley 1/4/62.

CONDEMNED:
1/10/62.
Cut–up Doncaster Works.

60124
KENILWORTH *from 8/50.*

Doncaster 2041.

To traffic 23/3/49.

REPAIRS:
Don.12/7–16/8/50.**G.**
Gat.19–20/3/51.**C/L.**
Gat.24–26/9/51.**C/L.**
Don.14/11–17/12/51.**H/I.**
Don.24–27/12/51.**N/C.**
Don.8–22/1/52.**N/C.**
Don.25/7–29/8/52.**C/L.**
Don.27/7–25/8/53.**G.**
Don.23/2–23/3/55.**G.**
Don.21/7–16/8/55.**C/L.**
Dar.18–25/11/55.**C/L.**
Don.20/9–19/10/56.**G.**
Don.25–30/10/56.**N/C.**
Don.6–23/2/57.**C/H.**
Don.18–30/3/57.**C/L.**
Don.15/4–16/5/58.**G.**
Don.20/1–12/2/59.**C/L.**
Don.9/7–12/8/59.**G.**
Don.19–22/8/59.**N/C.**
Don.17/1–1/3/61.**G.**
Don.22/4–5/5/61.**C/L.**
Don.29/8–29/9/61.**N/C.**
Dar.13/2–13/5/64.**G.**
Dar.20/8/65.*Weigh.*
Dar.17/12/65–1/1/66.**C/L.**

BOILERS:
9670 *Renumbered 29861 17/12/51.*
29817 (ex60138) 25/8/53.
29850 (ex60139) 23/3/55.
29856 (ex60135) 19/10/56.
29815 (ex60132) 16/5/58.

WORKS CODES:– Cow – Cowlairs. Dar – Darlington. Don – Doncaster. Gat – Gateshead. Hay – Haymarket Shed. Inv – Inverurie.

REPAIR CODES:– **C/H** – Casual Heavy. **C/L** – Casual Light. **G** – General. **H** – Heavy. **H/I** – Heavy Intermediate. **L** – Light. **L/I** – Light Intermediate. **N/C** – Non–Classified.

The horrific double collision at Harrow in 1952 considerably speeded development of train control but it took a further seven years to ensure a reliable Automatic Warning System. Track equipment for it on main lines gradually spread northwards and all the A1s were fitted for its use. 60162 did all its scheduled work from Haymarket shed in Edinburgh but here on 24th November 1961 was caught leaving Peterborough North station on a down express, subsequent to a general repair.

All the A1 Pacifics were fitted originally with electric lighting equipment, the Stone's turbo–generator for it being inside the right hand smoke deflector. Note the type of lamp irons adopted for it, and the outer ones on the buffer beam had grab handles on them. 60150 is at Peterborough on 26th November 1955 and did not then have Automatic Train Control apparatus fitted.

During the 1950s at least ten A1s had the electric lighting equipment removed completely, 60117 losing it by February 1953 when, as seen here, it was fitted with Automatic Train Control apparatus. The lighting was a mixed blessing, through the extra maintenance involved and oil lamps still had to be employed to denote the type of train to signalmen.

When new, none of the class were named, but when the first engine was two and a half months old it was in works for eight days to be fitted with nameplates. W.P. Allen was the Trades Union member of the Railway Executive, starting on the Great Northern Railway as a cleaner and progressing to driver. On 28th October 1948 this engine was named officially for him at a ceremony in Kings Cross station.

In the general naming which took place from April 1950, four of the A1s were named after LNER constitutent companies, the plates surmounted by the appropriate coat of arms. These had to be hand painted for which just one man at Doncaster then had the required skill; application began in June 1951 for *NORTH BRITISH* and was only completed with *GREAT CENTRAL* in July 1952.

60124 Continued

29863 (ex60136) 12/8/59.
29851 (ex60152) 1/3/61.
29807 (ex60145) 13/5/64.

SHEDS:
Gateshead.
Heaton 11/9/60.
York 10/9/61.
Darlington 22/11/64.

CONDEMNED:
27/3/66.
Sold for scrap 5/66 to
A.Draper, Hull.

60125
SCOTTISH UNION *from*
1/51.

Doncaster 2043.

To traffic 22/4/49.

REPAIRS:
Don.26–29/4/49.**N/C.**
Don.28/12/50–25/1/51.**G.**
Don.1/9–31/10/52.**G.**
Don.22/4–25/5/54.**G.**
Don.2–4/6/54.**N/C.**
Don.23/7–10/8/54.**N/C.**
Don.31/8–14/10/55.**G.**
Don.12–24/3/56.**N/C.**
Don.28/2–29/3/57.**G.**
Don.25/9–29/10/58.**G.**
Don.4–11/11/58.**N/C.**
Don.22/9–3/11/59.**C/L.**
Don.14/5–16/6/60.**G.**
Don.12/12/61–19/1/62.**G.**
Don.28/5/63.*Weigh.*

BOILERS:
9671 *Renumbered 29821*
25/1/51.
29831 (ex60154) 31/10/52.
29875 (New) 25/5/54.
29817 (ex60124) 14/10/55.
29814 (ex60530) 29/3/57.
29842 (ex60150) 29/10/58.
29858 (ex60128) 16/6/60.
29787 (ex60161) 19/1/62.

SHEDS:
Doncaster.
Copley Hill 4/6/50.
Grantham 15/2/53.
Copley Hill 7/6/53.
Grantham 2/5/54.
Kings Cross 16/6/57.
Doncaster 6/1/58.

CONDEMNED:
4/7/64.
Sold for scrap 8/64 to Cox
& Danks, Wadsley Bridge.

60126
SIR VINCENT RAVEN
from 8/50.

Doncaster 2042.

To traffic 27/4/49.

REPAIRS:
Don.7/6–28/7/50.**G.**
Don.7/9–17/10/51.**H/I.**
Don.5/11–5/12/52.**G.**
Gat.20–24/4/53.**C/L.**
Gat.27/10–4/11/53.**C/L.**
Don.5/2–16/3/54.**G.**
Don.1/9–1/10/54.**C/L.**
Gat.28/4–4/5/55.**C/L.**
Don.12–19/8/55.**C/L.**
Don.27/10–30/11/55.**G.**
Don.22/5–5/7/57.**G.**
Don.27/5–4/6/58.**N/C.**
Don.7/3–18/4/59.**G.**
Don.6–15/10/59.**N/C.**
Don.22/4–26/5/60.**C/L.**
Don.28/3–6/5/61.**G.**
Don.21/7–9/8/61.**C/L.**

BOILERS:
9672 *Renumbered 29852*
17/10/51.
29808 (ex60131) 5/12/52.
29832 (ex60531) 16/3/54.
29820 (ex60505) 30/11/55.
29811 (ex60137) 5/7/57.
29878 (ex60118) 18/4/59.
29882 (New) 6/5/61.

SHEDS:
Heaton.
York 10/9/61.

CONDEMNED:
18/1/65.
Sold for scrap 3/65 to
A.Draper,Hull.

60127
WILSON WORDSELL
from 9/50.

Doncaster 2044.

To traffic 13/5/49.

REPAIRS:
Don.17–19/5/49.**N/C.**
Don.2/8–13/9/50.**G.**
Don.19/2–26/3/52.**H/I.**
Gat.13–20/11/52.**N/C.**
Don.22–31/1/53.**N/C.**
Don.4/12/53–6/1/54.**G.**
Don.9–22/3/54.**N/C.**
Don.13/7–22/8/55.**G.**
Don.18/12/56–19/1/57.**G.**
Don.20/5–1/7/58.**G.**
Don.11/9–16/10/59.**G.**
Don.18/10–25/11/61.**G.**
Dar.7/10/63.*Weigh.*

BOILERS:
9673.
10636 (New) 13/9/50.
10636 *Renumbered 29866*
26/3/52.
29819 (ex60140) 6/1/54.
29810 (ex60144) 22/8/55.

29864 (ex60151) 19/1/57.
29782 (ex60519) 1/7/58.
29866 (ex60141) 16/10/59.
29789 (ex60537) 25/11/61.

SHEDS:
Heaton.
Tweedmouth 9/9/62.
Gateshead 18/10/64.

CONDEMNED:
14/6/65.
Sold for scrap 7/65 to
Hughes, Bolckow, Blyth.

60128
BONGRACE *from 11/50.*

Doncaster 2045.

To traffic 19/5/49.

REPAIRS:
Don.15–16/8/49.**N/C.**
Don.22/9/49.**N/C.**
Don.27–28/10/49.**N/C.**
Don.30/10–29/11/50.**H/I.**
Don.5/1–4/2/52.**G.**
Don.6–7/5/52.*Special*
Exam.
Don.16/12/52–22/1/53.**G.**
Don.25/2–11/3/53.**C/L.**
Don.15/7–14/8/53.**C/L.**
Don.24/8–30/9/54.**G.**
Don.25/11/55–4/1/56.**G.**
Don.26/1–1/2/56.**N/C.**
Don.1/5–5/6/57.**G.**
Don.25/8–16/10/58.**G.**
Don.14/3–30/4/60.**G.**
Don.11/3–21/4/61.**C/L.**
Don.31/8–13/10/61.**C/L.**
Don.7/5/62.*Weigh.*
Don.8/8–2/10/62.**G.**
Don.27–28/5/63.*Weigh.*

BOILERS:
9674 *Renumbered 29814*
29/11/50.
29871 (New) 4/2/52.
29834 (ex60123) 22/1/53.
29877 (New) 30/9/54.
29805 (ex60146) 5/6/57.
29858 (ex60155) 16/10/58.
29837 (ex60134) 30/4/60.
29868 (ex60146) 2/10/62.

SHEDS:
Copley Hill.
Kings Cross 4/6/50.
Grantham 9/9/51.
Kings Cross 15/9/57.
Doncaster 5/4/59.

CONDEMNED:
10/1/65.
Sold for scrap 2/65 to
A.Draper, Hull.

60129
GUY MANNERING *from*
11/50.

Doncaster 2046.

To traffic 15/6/49.

REPAIRS:
Gat.8–15/5/50.**C/L.**
Don.11/10–10/11/50.**H/I.**
Dar.22/1/51.*Weigh.*
Don.28/1–27/2/52.**G.**
Don.1/6–8/7/53.**G.**
Don.5/10–9/11/54.**G.**
Gat.11–15/7/55.**N/C.**
Don.31/1/56.*Weigh.*
Don.11/4–16/5/56.**G.**
Don.30/10–30/11/57.**G.**
Don.5–13/8/58.**N/C.**
Don.28/7–2/9/59.**G.**
Don.10/2–17/3/61.**G.**
Don.18–28/9/61.**N/C.**
Don.3–6/10/61.**N/C.**
Don.19/1–24/2/62.**C/L.**
Dar.25/9–7/12/63.**G.**
Dar.9–12/12/63.**N/C.**

BOILERS:
9675 *Renumbered 29812*
10/11/50.
29814 (ex60128) 27/2/52.
29800 (ex60143) 8/7/53.
29862 (ex60145) 9/11/54.
29836 (ex60531) 16/5/56.
29779 (ex60518) 30/11/57.
29828 (ex60158) 2/9/59.
29780 (ex60534) 17/3/61.
29870 (ex60155) 7/12/63.

SHEDS:
York.
Gateshead 4/9/49.
Heaton 11/9/60.
Tweedmouth 9/9/62.
Gateshead 6/12/64.
York 11/7/65.

CONDEMNED:
11/10/65.
Sold for scrap 11/65 to
R.A.King,Norwich.

60130
KESTREL *from 7/50.*

Darlington 2049.

To traffic 28/9/48.

REPAIRS:
Don.30/12/48–13/1/49.**C/L.**
Dar.1–9/3/49.**C/L.**
Don.1/6–20/7/50.**G.**
Don.17/11–12/12/50.**C/L.**
Don.3–10/4/51.**C/L.**
Don.5/12/51–11/1/52.**H/I.**
Don.10/3/52.*Weigh.*
Don.14–16/10/52.**N/C.**
A.T.C. fitted.
Don.14/1–11/2/53.**G.**
Don.26/2–2/3/53.**N/C.**
Don.1–11/3/54.**C/L.**
Don.27/4–18/5/54.**C/L.**
Don.22/11–23/12/54.**G.**

WORKS CODES:– Cow – Cowlairs. Dar – Darlington. Don – Doncaster. Gat – Gateshead. Hay – Haymarket Shed. Inv – Inverurie.

REPAIR CODES:– **C/H** – Casual Heavy. **C/L** – Casual Light. **G** – General. **H** – Heavy. **H/I** – Heavy Intermediate. **L** – Light. **L/I** – Light Intermediate. **N/C** – Non–Classified.

60157, during its long idle hours as up main line pilot at the south end of Doncaster station, in November 1964, only two months prior to its demise. By 1964 any pride in the appearance of the A1 class had been lost completely, even for those specially named. Almost all their main line work had been taken by the Deltics and their condition – at least outwardly – sadly deteriorated, as this illustrates.

Don.18–24/1/55.**N/C.**
A.T.C gear re–fitted.
Don.26/4/55.**N/C.**
Don.13/2/56.Weigh.
Don.30/10–29/11/56.**G.**
Don.18–20/6/57.**N/C.**
Don.27/7–6/8/57.**C/L.**
Don.25/10–15/11/57.**C/L.**
Don.14/6–29/7/58.**G.**
Don.19–27/11/59.**N/C.**
Don.25/5–16/7/60.**G.**
Don.31/12/62–13/2/63.**G.**

BOILERS:
3909 Renumbered 29863
11/1/52.
29847 (ex60511) 11/2/53.
29849 (ex60525) 23/12/54.
29859 (ex60119) 29/11/56.
29871 (ex60142) 29/7/58.
29805 (ex60159) 16/7/60.
29785 (ex60151) 13/2/63.

SHEDS:
Doncaster.
Kings Cross 17/10/48.
Grantham 9/9/51.
Ardsley 15/2/53.
Copley Hill 15/9/57.
Ardsley 6/9/64.

CONDEMNED:
4/10/65.
Sold for scrap 12/65 to
J.Cashmore, Great Bridge.

60131
OSPREY from 6/50.

Darlington 2050.

To traffic 5/10/48.

REPAIRS:
Don.24/2–10/3/49.**C/L.**
Don.24/10–3/11/49.**C/L.**
Don.7/12/49–3/1/50.**C/L.**
Don.1/5–16/6/50.**G.**
Don.25/9–12/10/50.**C/L.**
Don.21/8–28/9/51.**H/I.**
Don.13/10–13/11/52.**G.**
Don.9–15/2/53.**N/C.**
A.T.C. fitted.
Don.29/4–2/6/54.**G.**
Don.13/4/55.**N/C.**
Don.16–28/9/55.**C/L.**
Don.22/3–3/5/56.**G.**
Don.8–19/7/57.**C/L.**
Don.12–15/8/57.**N/C.**
Don.26–30/8/57.**N/C.**
Don.23–27/9/57.**N/C.**
Don.18/2–19/3/58.**G.**
Don.26/10–27/11/59.**G.**
Don.13–21/10/60.**N/C.**
Don.27/7–17/11/62.**G.**
Dar.15/12/64–8/1/65.**C/L.**
Dar.29/1–8/3/65.**C/L.**

BOILERS:
3911 Renumbered 29808
12/10/50.

29828 (ex60158) 13/11/52.
29831 (ex60125) 2/6/54.
29808 (ex60123) 19/3/58.
29779 (ex60129) 27/11/59.

SHEDS:
Kings Cross.
Grantham 9/9/51.
Copley Hill 15/2/53.
Ardsley 1/4/62.
Neville Hill 28/7/63.

CONDEMNED:
4/10/65.
Sold for scrap 11/65 to
T.W.Ward, Killamarsh.

60132
MARMION from 12/50.

Darlington 2051.

To traffic 18/10/48.

REPAIRS:
Don.22/9–3/11/49.**G.**
Dar.5/4/50.Weigh.
Dar.11/9/50.Weigh.
Don.23/11–22/12/50.**H/I.**
Dar.31/1/51.Weigh.
Gat.15–19/10/51.**C/L.**
Don.4/2–6/3/52.**G.**
Don.11/6–15/7/53.**G.**
Don.29/6–21/7/54.**C/L.**
Don.9/3–19/4/55.**G.**

Gat.17–23/5/55.**C/L.**
Don.24/9–26/10/56.**G.**
Don.17/3–22/4/58.**G.**
Don.6/10–12/11/59.**G.**
Don.22–24/8/60.**N/C.**
A.W.S. fitted.
Don.11/8–28/9/61.**G.**
Dar.28/11–19/12/63.**C/L.**
Dar.13–30/1/64.**C/L.**

BOILERS:
3913 Renumbered 29817
22/12/50.
29865 (ex60145) 6/3/52.
29814 (ex60129) 15/7/53.
29812 (ex60138) 19/4/55.
29815 (ex60533) 26/10/56.
29834 (ex60525) 22/4/58.
29836 (ex60156) 12/11/59.
29811 (ex60158) 28/9/61.

SHEDS:
Gateshead.
Heaton 15/5/60.
Tweedmouth 9/9/62.
Gateshead 6/12/64.

CONDEMNED:
14/6/65.
Sold for scrap 7/65 to
Hughes,Bolckow, Blyth.

60133
POMMERN from 4/50.

60116, leaving Leeds (Central) in 1956, has the *Queen of Scots Pullman* for Edinburgh and Glasgow. One of Heaton's top link performers, even from new this engine differed from all the others; it had the smokebox number plate in the normal place but with the cross–rail *above* it.

60146 in Leeds (Central) station in May 1962, on a running in turn back to Doncaster, following its final general repair. Note that it is one of those from which the electric lighting equipment was removed.

60133 Continued

Darlington 2052.

To traffic 30/10/48.

REPAIRS:
Dar.15–28/11/48.**C/L.**
Dar.19/2–11/3/49.**C/L.**
Don.15–23/9/49.**C/L.**
Don.6/2–12/4/50.**G.**
Don.6–9/11/50.**C/L.**
Don.12/1–9/2/51.**H/I.**
Don.20/5–19/6/52.**G.**
Don.4–16/7/52.**N/C.**
Don.20–25/2/53.**N/C.**
Don.17/3–15/4/54.**H/I.**
Don.22/2–18/3/55.**G.**
Don.22/7–24/8/55.**G.**
Don.12/11/56.*Weigh.*
Don.4–19/1/57.**C/L.**
Don.17/5–4/7/57.**G.**
Don.14/5–19/6/59.**G.**
Don.29/2–2/3/60.**C/L.**
Don.28/4–12/5/60.**N/C.**
Don.9–21/1/61.**N/C.**
Don.17/2–1/4/61.**H/I.**
Don.17/9–22/10/62.**N/C.**
Dar.25/3–15/5/64.**C/L.**

BOILERS:
3917 *Renumbered 29826 9/2/51.*
29824 (ex60155) 19/6/52.
29863 (ex60143) 24/8/55.
29812 (ex60132) 4/7/57.
29838 (ex60151) 19/6/59.

SHEDS:
Grantham.
Copley Hill 4/6/50.
Ardsley 6/9/54.

CONDEMNED:
21/6/65.
Sold for scrap 8/65 to
Clayton & Davie,
Dunston.

60134
FOXHUNTER from 10/50.

Darlington 2053.

To traffic 5/11/48.

REPAIRS:
Don.3/1–3/3/50.**G.**
Don.9–13/10/50.**C/L.**
Don.22/5–21/6/51.**G.**
Don.22–29/10/51.**C/L.**
Don.6/1–6/2/53.**H/I.**
Don.10/8–17/9/54.**H/I.**
Don.8/11/54.**N/C.**
Don.28/5–7/7/56.**G.**
Don.24/1–13/2/57.**C/H.**
Don.28/4–29/5/58.**G.**
Don.5–14/2/59.**N/C.**
Don.7–22/10/59.**N/C.**
Don.22/2–30/3/60.**G.**
Don.1–17/1/62.**C/L.**
Don.10/8–16/10/62.**G.**
Don.25/3–30/4/63.**C/L.**

BOILERS:
3919.
29842 (New) 21/6/51.

29835 (ex60155) 7/7/56.
29837 (ex60537) 29/5/58.
29839 (ex60121) 30/3/60.
29801 (ex60532) 16/10/62.

SHEDS:
Copley Hill.
Ardsley 1/4/62.
Neville Hill 28/7/63.

CONDEMNED:
4/10/65.
Sold for scrap 11/65 to
T.W.Ward, Beighton.

60135
MADGE WILDFIRE from 10/50.

Darlington 2054.

To traffic 18/11/48.

REPAIRS:
Dar.2–12/8/49.**N/C.**
Dar.22/9–3/12/49.**C/H.**
Dar.12/4/50.*Weigh.*
Gat.17–23/5/50.**C/L.**
Gat.29/6–4/7/50.**C/L.**
Don.30/8–6/10/50.**G.**
Gat.13–19/3/51.**C/L.**
Don.4/6–1/8/51.**H/I.**
Don.7/11–11/12/52.**G.**
Don.19/10–11/11/53.**C/L.**
Don.28/7–31/8/54.**G.**
Don.4/1–4/2/56.**G.**
Don.28/5–12/7/57.**G.**
Don.2–11/6/58.**N/C.**
Don.21/10–3/12/58.**G.**
Don.9–21/2/59.**C/L.**
Don.4/8–14/9/60.**G.**

BOILERS:
3922.
29803 (ex60138) 6/10/50.
29838 (ex60152) 11/12/52.
29856 (ex60515) 31/8/54.
29819 (ex60127) 4/2/56.
29877 (ex60128) 12/7/57.
29876 (ex60501) 3/12/58.
29842 (ex60125) 14/9/60.

SHEDS:
Gateshead.
Copley Hill 20/11/60.
Ardsley 1/4/62.

CONDEMNED:
12/11/62.
Into Doncaster Works for
cut–up 17/5/63.

60136
ALCAZAR from 12/50.

Darlington 2055.

To traffic 26/11/48.

REPAIRS:
Don.19/10–21/12/49.**C/H.**
Don.15–19/5/50.**N/C.**
A.T.C. fitted.
Don.30–31/10/50.**N/C.**
Don.9/11–8/12/50.**H/I.**

Don.26/11/51–17/1/52.**G.**
Don.23/3–24/4/53.**G.**
Don.20/7/53.*Weigh.*
Don.13/7–17/8/54.**G.**
Don.30/11/54.*Weigh.*
Don.13/12/55–16/1/56.**G.**
Don.24/10–3/11/56.**N/C.**
Don.4/6–19/7/57.**G.**
Don.24/7–2/8/57.**N/C.**
Don.12–21/11/57.**N/C.**
Don.30/11–4/12/57.**C/L.**
Don.21–30/4/58.**C/L.**
Don.3–6/5/58.**N/C.**
Don.9–11/3/59.**N/C.**
Don.22/4–22/5/59.**G.**
Don.20–27/7/60.**N/C.**
Don.13/2–25/3/61.**G.**
Don.18–21/4/61.**N/C.**
Don.24/4–2/5/61.**C/L.**

BOILERS:
3924 *Renumbered 29815 8/12/50.*
29846 (ex60162) 24/4/53.
29844 (ex60539) 16/1/56.
29863 (ex60133) 19/7/57.
29861 (ex60144) 22/5/59.
29784 (ex60514) 25/3/61.

SHEDS:
Copley Hill.
Kings Cross 21/5/50.
Grantham 9/9/51.
Kings Cross 7/4/57.
Doncaster 6/4/58.
Kings Cross 3/8/58.
Doncaster 5/4/59.

CONDEMNED:
22/5/63.
Into Doncaster Works for
cut–up 29/5/63.

60137
REDGAUNTLET from 6/50.

Darlington 2056.

To traffic 3/12/48.

REPAIRS:
Dar.16/5–1/6/49.**C/L.**
Dar.21/11–21/12/49.**C/L.**
Don.25/4–9/6/50.**G.**
Gat.20–24/4/51.**C/L.**
Don.22/5–12/7/51.**G.**
Don.14/11–4/12/51.**C/L.**
Don.12–15/5/52.**N/C.**
Gat.2–11/12/52.**N/C.**
Don.9/2–6/3/53.**G.**
Gat.7–12/11/54.**C/L.**
Don.11/5–2/7/54.**G.**
Don.6–9/7/54.**N/C.**
Don.21/9–1/11/55.**G.**
Gat.28/8–3/9/56.**C/L.**
Don.10–15/12/56.**C/L.**
Don.21/3–26/4/57.**G.**
Don.1–30/5/58.**C/L.**
Don.11/11/58–1/1/59.**G.**
Don.23/7–26/8/60.**G.**
Don.29/4–31/5/61.**C/L.**

BOILERS:
3926.

29843 (ex60532) 12/7/51.
29851 (ex60515) 6/3/53.
29827 (ex60160) 2/7/54.
29811 (ex60120) 1/11/55.
29817 (ex60125) 26/4/57.
29877 (ex60135) 1/1/59.
29846 (ex60123) 26/8/60.

SHEDS:
Gateshead.
Heaton 15/5/60.
Tweedmouth 9/9/62.

CONDEMNED:
29/10/62.
Into Doncaster Works for
cut–up 16/4/63.

60138
BOSWELL from 9/50.

Darlington 2057.

To traffic 10/12/48.

REPAIRS:
Don.26/8–27/9/49.**C/L.**
Dar.10/2–10/3/50.**C/L.**
Don.14/8–21/9/50.**G.**
Don.12/3–9/4/52.**G.**
Don.13/7–14/8/53.**G.**
Don.4/3/54.**N/C.**
Don.1–16/11/54.**N/C.**
Don.28/2–30/3/55.**G.**
Don.23/5–7/6/55.**C/L.**
Don.20/7–23/8/56.**C/L.**
Don.21/9–2/10/56.**C/L.**
Don.2/5–8/6/57.**G.**
Don.7/3–22/4/59.**G.**
Don.13–20/8/60.**N/C.**
Don.24/2–28/3/61.**C/L.**
Don.1/12/61–13/1/62.**G.**
Dar.6–10/1/64.**C/L.**

BOILERS:
3928.
29801 (ex60143) 21/9/50.
29817 (ex60132) 9/4/52.
29812 (ex60526) 14/8/53.
29866 (ex60537) 30/3/55.
29833 (ex60154) 8/6/57.
29819 (ex60162) 22/4/59.
29816 (ex60525) 13/1/62.

SHED:
York.

CONDEMNED:
4/10/65.
Sold for scrap 11/65 to
T.W.Ward, Killamarsh.

60139
SEA EAGLE from 5/50.

Darlington 2058.

To traffic 23/12/48.

REPAIRS:
Dar.9–19/1/49.**C/L.**
Don.17/4–26/5/50.**G.**
Don.30–31/5/50.**N/C.**
Don.6–9/6/50.**N/C.**
Don.2–5/10/50.**C/L.**

Don.18/8–25/9/51.**G.**
Don.6–25/2/52.**C/L.**
Don.29/1–4/2/53.**N/C.**
A.T.C. fitted.
Don.4/5–5/6/53.**H/I.**
Don.21/12/53–26/1/54.**C/L.**
Don.9/2–12/3/55.**G.**
Don.4/10–9/11/56.**G.**
Don.26/1–2/2/57.**N/C.**
Don.19/6–1/8/58.**G.**
Don.8–13/8/58.**N/C.**
Don.21/11–9/12/58.**C/L.**
Don.16–28/5/59.**C/L.**
Don.6–7/1/60.**N/C.**
Don.26/2–1/4/60.**G.**
Don.3–4/11/60.**N/C.**
Don.13/1/61.*Weigh.*
Don.13–25/2/61.**C/L.**
Don.13/2–31/3/62.**G.**
Dar.18/10–30/11/63.**C/L.**
After collision.

BOILERS:
3930.
29850 (ex60149) 25/9/51.
29839 (ex60117) 12/3/55.
29862 (ex60129) 9/11/56.
29785 (ex60115) 1/8/58.
29786 (ex60505) 1/4/60.
29858 (ex60125) 31/3/62.

SHEDS:
Kings Cross.
Copley Hill 15/7/51.
Grantham 18/12/55.
Kings Cross 7/4/57.
Doncaster 5/4/59.

CONDEMNED:
7/6/64.
Sold for scrap 1/65 to Cox
& Danks, Wadsley Bridge.

60140
BALMORAL from 7/50.

Darlington 2059.

To traffic 24/12/48.

REPAIRS:
Dar.7–8/2/49.**N/C.**
Dar.2–9/6/49.**C/L.**
Don.22/5–5/7/50.**G.**
Don.25/10–23/11/51.**G.**
Don.9–18/12/52.**N/C.**
Don.11/11–11/12/53.**G.**
Don.17–24/5/54.**C/L.**
Don.28/10–19/11/54.**C/L.**
Don.24/10–25/11/55.**G.**
Don.4/12/57–3/1/58.**G.**
Don.19–28/5/58.**N/C.**
Don.25/6–19/7/58.**C/L.**
Don.10/12/59–19/1/60.**G.**
Don.20–23/7/60.**N/C.**
Don.16–2–11/3/61.**C/L.**
Don.8/5–4/7/62.**G.**

BOILERS:
3931.
29819 (ex60144) 23/11/51.

29822 (ex60531) 11/12/53.
29813 (ex60118) 25/11/55.
29802 (ex60156) 3/1/58.
29808 (ex60131) 19/1/60.
29806 (ex60119) 4/7/62.

SHEDS:
York.
Kings Cross 9/10/49.
York 4/6/50.

CONDEMNED:
11/1/65.
Sold for scrap 3/65 to
A.Draper, Hull.

60141
ABBOTSFORD from 5/50.

Darlington 2060.

To traffic 31/12/48.

REPAIRS:
Dar.9–12/2/49.**C/L.**
Dar.2–20/5/49.**C/L.**
Don.6/2–3/5/50.**G.**
Don.13–24/11/50.**C/L.**
Don.5–22/1/51.**C/L.**
Don.7/8–19/9/51.**H/I.**
Don.16/2–17/3/53.**G.**
Don.27/9–26/10/54.**G.**
Don.20/2–28/3/56.**G.**
Don.19/9–18/10/57.**G.**
Don.16/3/59.*Weigh.*
Don.3/7–7/8/59.**G.**
Don.22/3–28/4/61.**G.**
Dar.20/11/63.**N/C.**

BOILERS:
3934 *Renumbered 29849
19/9/51.*
29843 (ex60137) 17/3/53.
29834 (ex60128) 26/10/54.
29828 (ex60143) 28/3/56.
29866 (ex60138) 18/10/57.
29812 (ex60133) 7/8/59.
29883 (New) 28/4/61.

SHEDS:
York.
Kings Cross 9/10/49.
Copley Hill 21/5/50.
York 8/9/63.

CONDEMNED:
5/10/64.
Sold for scrap 12/64 to
A.Draper, Hull.

60142
*EDWARD FLETCHER
from 10/50.*

Darlington 2061.

To traffic 2/2/49.

REPAIRS:
Dar.22/8/49.*Weigh.*
Don.12/9–18/10/50.**G.**

Don.6/11–12/12/51.**H/I.**
Don.6–11/11/52.**N/C.**
Don.16/1–14/2/53.**G.**
Gat.4–8/9/53.**N/C.**
Don.30/9–27/10/53.**C/L.**
Don.2/6–14/7/54.**H/I.**
Don.26/3–8/5/56.**G.**
Don.12/2–12/3/58.**G.**
Don.26/10–20/11/59.**G.**
Don.22–25/8/60.**N/C.**
Don.12/6–21/7/61.**G.**

BOILERS:
3943.
29805 (ex60135) 18/10/50.
29871 (ex60128) 14/2/53.
29823 (ex60161) 12/3/58.
29782 (ex60127) 20/11/59.
29828 (ex60129) 21/7/61.

SHEDS:
Gateshead.
Heaton 11/9/60.
Tweedmouth 9/9/62.
Gateshead 25/10/64.

CONDEMNED:
14/6/65.
Sold for scrap 7/65 to
Hughes,Bolckow, Blyth.

60143
*SIR WALTER SCOTT from
9/50.*

Darlington 2062.

To traffic 22/2/49.

REPAIRS:
Dar.16/8/49.*Weigh.*
Don.3–19/10/49.**C/L.**
Dar.10/11/49.*Weigh.*
Don.16/1–1/2/50.**C/L.**
Don.10/8–15/9/50.**G.**
Don.18/9–18/10/51.**H/I.**
Don.23/1–25/2/53.**G.**
Don.10/5–15/6/54.**G.**
Don.12/10–16/11/55.**G.**
Gat.14–26/2/57.**C/L.**
Don.16/2–20/7/57.**G.**
Don.11–19/3/58.**N/C.**
Don.11/8–2/9/58.**C/H.**
Don.5/6–15/7/59.**G.**
Don.10/4–19/5/61.**G.**

BOILERS:
3944.
29800 (ex60127) 15/9/50.
29863 (ex60130) 25/2/53.
29828 (ex60131) 15/6/54.
29875 (ex60125) 16/11/55.
29827 (ex60152) 20/7/57.
29862 (ex60139) 2/9/58.
29847 (ex60506) 15/7/59.
29850 (ex60157) 19/5/61.

SHEDS:
Gateshead.
Heaton 15/5/60.

Tweedmouth 9/9/62.
York 8/9/63.

CONDEMNED:
6/5/64.
Sold for scrap 7/64 to
A.Draper, Hull.

60144
*KING'S COURIER from
1/51.*

Darlington 2063.

To traffic 2/3/49.

REPAIRS:
Don.14/6–7/7/50.**C/L.**
Don.7/12/50–9/1/51.**H/I.**
Don.25/9–31/10/51.**G.**
Don.28/4–1/6/53.**G.**
Don.16/7/53.*Weigh.*
Don.23/3–13/4/54.**C/H.**
Don.14/2–16/3/55.**G.**
Don.9/11–2/12/55.**C/L.**
Don.16/1–10/2/56.**C/H.**
Don.16/2–21/3/57.**G.**
Don.1/8/57.*Weigh.*
Don.15–24/9/58.**N/C.**
Don.19–23/1/59.**N/C.**
Don.13/3–23/4/59.**G.**
Don.16/9/59.*Weigh.*
Don.14/11–19/12/60.**G.**
Don.23–30/3/61.**C/L.**

BOILERS:
3945 *Renumbered 29819
9/1/51.*
29854 (ex60139) 31/10/51.
29810 (ex60533) 1/6/53.
29873 (ex60155) 16/3/55.
29861 (ex60116) 21/3/57.
29820 (ex60145) 23/4/59.
29814 (ex60114) 19/12/60.

SHEDS:
Doncaster.
Copley Hill 18/12/49.
Kings Cross 4/6/50.
Copley Hill 15/7/51.
Ardsley 9/9/51.
Grantham 15/2/53.
Kings Cross 15/9/57.
Doncaster 10/11/57.

CONDEMNED:
30/4/63.
Into Doncaster Works for
cut–up 9/5/63.

60145
SAINT MUNGO from 8/50.

Darlington 2064.

To traffic 23/3/49.

REPAIRS:
Dar.19/4/50.*Weigh.*
Don.17/7–23/8/50.**G.**
Don.29/11/51–1/1/52.**G.**

WORKS CODES:– Cow – Cowlairs. Dar – Darlington. Don – Doncaster. Gat – Gateshead. Hay – Haymarket Shed. Inv – Inverurie.

REPAIR CODES:– **C/H** – Casual Heavy. **C/L** – Casual Light. **G** – General. **H** – Heavy. **H/I** – Heavy Intermediate. **L** – Light. **L/I** – Light Intermediate. **N/C** – Non–Classified.

60119 at Wortley South on a goods to Doncaster, in 1955. It was a Leeds engine until the end of that year, having received its Automatic Train Control apparatus during February 1953. From January 1954 smokebox number plates were refitted across the upper door hinge strap so that the top lamp iron could be moved 6 ¼ inches lower to make it easier to mount a lamp or headboard on it. The cross rail was not moved so that on all engines it was then above the number plate.

60125 photographed at Kings Cross station on 19th February 1962, heading an express it will work to Doncaster. From December 1961 the top lamp iron on 21 of the A1 class was moved down still further and to allow this the cross–rail had to be split into short lengths, on either side of the iron.

60121 on Saturday 17th August 1963 arrived in Scarborough on the through holiday train from Glasgow, avoiding York by leaving the main line at Pilmoor and then performing a complicated double reversal east of Malton station. Here it is assisting the Scarborough station pilot to dispose of the coaches; it would then run tender first to its home (and only) shed of York because it could not be turned at Scarborough.

60122 in June 1958, threading the tunnels at Welwyn on a Kings Cross working whilst it was shedded there, from September 1957 until April 1958.

In September 1953 No. 60126 is coming off the High Level Bridge and going west through Newcastle Central station, on a Heaton shed class D goods duty.

When displaced by diesels in 1962 Heaton sent some of its A1s to Tweedmouth shed where they proved useful cover for any wayward performance by diesels on the main line. Tweedmouth also had an all stations working to and from Edinburgh and 60127 is on it here, drawing up for the stop at East Fortune.

60131 has *The West Riding* **south of Potters Bar – in addition to taking the name from the pre-war streamliner its first five coaches are also a legacy from that luxurious train.**

Only six months old, 60132 in April 1949 leaving Edinburgh with the up *Flying Scotsman.* **Absence of a headboard was most unusual but the clock on the North British Hotel proves that it was the 10 o'clock departure. This engine was never fitted with Flaman speed recorder.**

Until February 1953 No. 60144 was seen mainly between Leeds and Kings Cross but then moved to Grantham from where it had regular York workings. With the Minster prominent in the background the location is easily identified.

60145 Continued

Don.11/3–17/4/53.**G.**
Don.2/9–12/10/54.**G.**
Don.7/2–9/3/56.**G.**
Don.2/9–5/10/57.**G.**
Don.24/9–2/10/58.**N/C.**
Don.17/12/58–24/1/59.**G.**
Don.21/12/59–12/1/60.**C/L.**
Don.10/11–23/12/60.**G.**
Don.27/8–4/10/62.**C/H.**
Dar.28/10/63–1/2/64.**G.**
Dar.15/9–22/10/64.**C/L.**

BOILERS:
3946.
29862 (ex60121) 1/1/52.
29837 (ex60501) 12/10/54.
29818 (ex60122) 9/3/56.
29820 (ex60126) 5/10/57.
29845 (ex60515) 24/1/59.
29807 (ex60501) 23/12/60.
29875 (exSpare) 1/2/64.

SHEDS:
Gateshead.
Copley Hill 20/11/60.
York 8/9/63.
Darlington 2/1/66.
York 17/4/66.

CONDEMNED:
19/6/66. *Originally withdrawn 27/3/66 but re-instated 17/4/66 and allocated to York.* Sold for scrap 8/66 to A.Draper, Hull.

60146
PEREGRINE *from 12/50.*

Darlington 2065.

To traffic 11/4/49.

REPAIRS:
Dar.25–28/4/49.**N/C.**
Don.13/11–15/12/50.**H/I.**
Don.1/11–4/12/51.**G.**
Don.28/4–27/5/52.**C/L.**
Don.6/2–13/3/53.**H/I.**
Don.29/11/54–6/1/55.**G.**
Don.18–19/1/55.*Weigh.*
Don.15/2/55.*Weigh.*
Don.17/6/55.*Weigh.*
Don.5/6/56.*Weigh.*
Don.17/11–28/12/56.**G.**
Don.14/3/57.*Weigh.*
Don.27/4–10/5/57.**N/C.**
Don.24–31/5/57.**N/C.**
Don.8–17/5/58.**C/L.**
Don.11–17/6/58.**N/C.**
Don.2–21/10/58.**C/H.**
Don.22–23/7/59.**N/C.**
Don.30/11–31/12/59.**G.**
Don.6–8/7/60.**N/C.**
Don.15/8–7/10/60.**C/L.**
Don.20–23/11/61.**N/C.**
Don.16/4–24/5/62.**G.**
Dar.31/1–14/3/64.**C/L.**

BOILERS:
3948 *Renumbered 29816 15/12/50.*
29859 (ex60140) 4/12/51.
29805 (ex60157) 6/1/55.
29849 (ex60130) 28/12/56.
29872 (ex60148) 21/10/58.
29868 (ex60519) 31/12/59.
29865 (ex60118) 24/5/62.

SHEDS:
Doncaster.
Copley Hill 30/4/50.
York 4/6/50.
Neville Hill 28/7/63.
York 13/10/63.

CONDEMNED:
4/10/65.
Sold for scrap 11/65 to T.W.Ward, Killamarsh.

60147
NORTH EASTERN *from 3/52.*

Darlington 2066.

To traffic 13/4/49.

REPAIRS:
Gat.10–17/10/49.**C/L.**
Don.12–30/5/50.**C/L.**
Don.25/10–29/11/50.**H/I.**
Don.30/7–29/8/51.**H/I.**
Don.11/2–10/3/52.**C/H.**
Don.6–27/5/52.**C/L.**
Don.9–22/12/52.**C/L.**
Don.18/5–17/6/53.**G.**
Don.3/11–3/12/54.**G.**
Don.19–26/4/55.**C/L.**
Don.13/3–20/4/56.**G.**
Don.21/10–16/11/57.**G.**
Don.22–31/7/58.**N/C.**
Don.14–21/2/59.**C/L.**
Don.19/11–18/12/59.**G.**
Don.3/7–11/8/61.**G.**

BOILERS:
3956 *Renumbered 29813 29/11/50.*
29825 (ex60539) 17/6/53.
29843 (ex60141) 3/12/54.
29838 (ex60161) 20/4/56.
29803 (ex60162) 16/11/57.
29823 (ex60142) 18/12/59.
29812 (ex60141) 11/8/61.

SHEDS:
Gateshead.
Heaton 11/9/60.
Tweedmouth 9/9/62.
York 8/9/63.

CONDEMNED:
28/8/64.
Sold for scrap 11/64 to A.Draper, Hull.

60148
ABOYEUR *from 1/51.*

Darlington 2067.

To traffic 25/5/49.

REPAIRS:
Dar.9–22/6/49.**N/C.**
Don.30/11/50–4/1/51.**H/I.**
Don.11–20/6/51.**C/L.**
Don.26/9–14/11/51.**C/L.**
Don.9/6–11/7/52.**G.**
Don.14/7/53.*Weigh.*
Don.21/9–22/10/53.**G.**
Don.28/4–3/6/55.**G.**
Don.30/8–17/10/56.**G.**
Don.25/8–9/10/58.**G.**
Don.27–30/1/59.**N/C.**
Don.23–29/4/59.**N/C.**
Don.27/7/59.*Weigh.*
Don.1–9/12/59.**N/C.**
Don.25/10–24/11/60.**G.**
Don.24/11–8/12/61.**N/C.**
Don.25/4–25/5/62.**C/L.**
Don.30/5–16/6/62.**C/L.**

BOILERS:
3957 *Renumbered 29818 4/1/51.*
29826 *(ex60133) 11/7/52.*
29874 *(ex60155) 22/10/53.*
29879 *(New) 3/6/55.*
29872 *(ex60115) 17/10/56.*
29810 *(ex60116) 9/10/58.*
29800 *(ex60153) 24/11/60.*

SHEDS:
Grantham.
Kings Cross 4/6/50.
Grantham 9/9/51,
Copley Hill 18/10/53.
Grantham 2/5/54.
Copley Hill 28/8/55.
Ardsley 6/9/64.
Gateshead 6/12/64.
Ardsley 3/1/65.

CONDEMNED:
21/6/65.
Sold for scrap 8/65 to Arnott,Young, Dinsdale.

60149
AMADIS *from 12/50.*

Darlington 2068.

To traffic 31/5/49.

REPAIRS:
Dar.20–23/6/49.**N/C.**
Don.29/9–10/10/49.**C/L.**
A.T.C. fitted.
Don.17–18/4/50.**N/C.**
Don.18/9–20/10/50.**G.**
Don.13/7–16/8/51.**H/I.**
Don.25/3–4/4/52.**N/C.**
Don.30/9–31/10/52.**G.**
Don.22/7/53.*Weigh.*
Don.26/10–24/11/53.**G.**
Don.15–22/12/53.**N/C.**
Don.11–17/1/55.**N/C.**
Don.29/3–10/5/55.**G.**

Don.3–11/5/56.**C/L.**
Don.23/7–23/8/56.**G.**
Don.8–10/7/57.**N/C.**
Don.6/5–11/6/58.**G.**
Don.7/11/58.*Weigh.*
Don.25/11–31/12/59.**G.**
Don.31/5–1/7/60.**C/L.**
Don.9/9–18/10/60.**C/L.**
Don.7/11–22/12/61.**G.**
Don.11/4/63.*Weigh.*

BOILERS:
3962.
29807 (ex60142) 20/10/50.
29822 (ex60531) 31/10/52.
29826 (ex60148) 24/11/53.
29785 (ex60519) 10/5/55.
29870 (ex60150) 23/8/56.
29856 (ex60124) 11/6/58.
29875 (ex60536) 31/12/59.
29823 (ex60147) 22/12/61.

SHEDS:
Grantham.
Kings Cross 10/10/49.
Grantham 19/3/50.
Kings Cross 19/4/50.
Grantham 9/9/51.
Kings Cross 16/9/56.
Doncaster 28/9/58.

CONDEMNED:
7/6/64.
Sold for scrap 1/65 to Cox & Danks, Wadsley Bridge.

60150
WILLBROOK *from 1/51.*

Darlington 2069.

To traffic 15/6/49.

REPAIRS:
Dar.9–14/7/49.**N/C.**
Dar.31/10–2/11/49.**N/C.**
Don.12/12/50–12/1/51.**H/I.**
Don.25/2–26/3/52.**G.**
Don.19/8–28/9/53.**G.**
Don.14/1–11/2/55.**G.**
Don.14/6–4/8/56.**G.**
Don.1/2–6/3/58.**G.**
Don.4/8–16/9/59.**G.**
Don.5/7–18/8/61.**G.**
Don.19–27/3/62.**C/L.**
Dar.30/1–5/2/64.**C/L.**

BOILERS:
3968 *Renumbered 29820 12/1/51.*
29873 *(New) 26/3/52.*
29861 *(ex60124) 28/9/53.*
29870 *(ex60156) 11/2/55.*
29842 *(ex60134) 4/8/56.*
29813 *(ex60140) 6/3/58.*
29822 *(ex60538) 16/9/59.*
29782 *(ex60142) 18/8/61.*

SHEDS:
Heaton.
Gateshead 10/7/49.

WORKS CODES:- Cow – Cowlairs. Dar – Darlington. Don – Doncaster. Gat – Gateshead. Hay – Haymarket Shed. Inv – Inverurie.

REPAIR CODES:- **C/H** – Casual Heavy. **C/L** – Casual Light. **G** – General. **H** – Heavy. **H/I** – Heavy Intermediate. **L** – Light. **L/I** – Light Intermediate. **N/C** – Non-Classified.

60135 stands by the weigh house in Doncaster works yard on 8th October 1950, at the conclusion of its first general repair, during which it was named and changed to blue painting. It kept its original chimney on this occasion but it was replaced by the cast type when in for a heavy repair in June/July 1951.

Any **Pacific at Hull Paragon station was noteworthy even if 60140 here, in 1961, is only pulling out with empty coaching stock. It would have worked in with the 3 a.m. mail and newspapers from Leeds, turning on the West Parade – Anlaby Road – Botanic Gardens triangle of lines before going back to Leeds.**

York 20/11/60.

CONDEMNED:
5/10/64.
Sold for scrap 12/64 to
A.Draper, Hull.

60151
MIDLOTHIAN from 3/51.

Darlington 2070.

To traffic 30/6/49.

REPAIRS:
Dar.12–15/7/49.**N/C.**
Gat.3–8/5/50.**C/L.**
Gat.22–26/6/50.**C/L.**
Don.15/1–2/3/51.**G.**
Don.7/5–11/6/52.**G.**
Don.7/8–4/9/53.**G.**
Don.28/3–5/5/55.**G.**
Don.13/7–15/8/56.**G.**
Don.7/1–6/2/58.**N/C.**
Don.13–22/5/58.**N/C.**
Don.24/3–1/5/59.**G.**
Don.2/8–14/9/60.**G.**
Don.22/11–21/12/61.**C/L.**
Don.29/8–2/11/62.**G.**
Don.20/12/62–10/1/63.**C/L.**
Don.5–12/2/63.**C/L.**
Don.20/6–11/7/63.**N/C.**
Dar.5–20/2/64.**C/L.**
Dar.3–21/4/64.**N/C.**

BOILERS:
3958.
29802 (New) 2/3/51.
29801 (ex60138) 11/6/52.
29864 (ex60118) 4/9/53.
29832 (ex60126) 15/8/56.
29838 (ex60147) 6/2/58.
29849 (ex60146) 1/5/59.
29785 (ex60139) 14/9/60.
29860 (ex60527) 2/11/62.

SHEDS:
Gateshead.
Heaton 15/5/60.
Tweedmouth 9/9/62.
Gateshead 18/10/64.
York 11/7/65.

CONDEMNED:
24/11/65.
Sold for scrap 1/66 to
Station Steel, Wath.

60152
HOLYROOD from 6/51.

Darlington 2071.

To traffic 8/7/49.

REPAIRS:
Don.15–23/6/50.**C/L.**
Dar.5/2/51.Weigh.
Don.30/4–1/6/51.**G.**
Cow.22–23/6/51.**N/C.**
Don.27/10–21/11/52.**G.**

Don.9/6–20/7/54.**H/I.**
Cow.28–30/4/55.**N/C.**
Don.7/11–17/12/55.**G.**
Don.6/5–15/6/57.**G.**
Don.1–4/7/57.**N/C.**
Don.2–16/5/58.**C/L.**
Don.3/12/58–16/1/59.**G.**
Don.1/11–13/12/60.**G.**
Don.22/5–9/6/62.**N/C.**
Don.21/3–23/5/63.**G.**

BOILERS:
3975 Renumbered 29838
1/6/51.
29841 (ex60161) 21/11/52.
29827 (ex60137) 17/12/55.
29865 (ex60528) 15/6/57.
29851 (ex60511) 16/1/59.
29827 (ex60117) 13/12/60.
29831 (ex60114) 23/5/63.

SHEDS:
Haymarket.
Polmadie 14/1/51.
Haymarket 11/3/51.
Polmadie 28/12/52.
Haymarket 29/6/53.
St Margarets 9/9/63.
York 6/9/64.

CONDEMNED:
21/6/65.
Sold for scrap 8/65 to
J.Cashmore, Great Bridge.

60153
FLAMBOYANT from 8/50.

Doncaster 2047.

To traffic 26/8/49.

REPAIRS:
Don.30/1–3/2/50.**C/L.**
Don.12–20/4/50.**C/L.**
Don.15/6–21/8/50.**C/H.**
After derailment.
Don.11/4/51.Weigh.
Don.3–13/7/51.**C/L.**
Don.3–21/9/51.**C/L.**
Don.25/10–4/12/51.**G.**
Don.24/7–1/8/52.**N/C.**
Don.29/9/52.Weigh.
Don.17–24/12/52.**N/C.**
Don.9/7–18/8/53.**G.**
Don.24/8–3/9/54.**C/L.**
Don.14/4–25/5/55.**G.**
Don.3/7/56.Axle test.
Don.18/3–24/4/57.**G.**
Don.9–12/12/57.**C/L.**
Don.16/9/58.Weigh.
Don.10–21/11/58.**C/L.**
Don.1/3–8/4/60.**G.**
Don.19/2–14/3/62.**N/C.**

BOILERS:
10590 Renumbered 29860
4/12/51.
29787 (ex60518) 25/5/55.
29800 (ex60121) 24/4/57.
29834 (ex60132) 8/4/60.

SHED:
York.

CONDEMNED:
2/11/62.
Into Doncaster Works for
cut–up 28/3/63.

60154
BON ACCORD from 4/51.

Doncaster 2048.

To traffic 23/9/49.

REPAIRS:
Don.19/12/49–6/1/50.**C/L.**
Don.20–27/4/50.**C/L.**
Don.7/3–18/4/51.**H/I.**
Don.7–9/5/51.**N/C.**
Don.10/7–15/8/52.**G.**
Don.12/11–19/12/53.**G.**
Don.18/10–15/11/54.**C/L.**
Gat.7–26/7/55.**N/C.**
Don.4/11–17/12/55.**G.**
Don.4–5/7/56.Axle test.
Don.22/11–7/12/56.**N/C.**
Don.21/3–27/4/57.**G.**
Don.12/8–26/9/58.**G.**
Don.21/8–1/9/59.**N/C.**
Don.22/3–4/5/60.**G.**
Don.3–16/11/61.**N/C.**
Don.18/9–12/11/62.**G.**
Dar.16–29/8/63.**C/L.**
Dar.28/10–4/11/63.**C/L.**
Dar.20/10–7/11/64.**C/L.**
Dar.9–10/11/64.**N/C.**

BOILERS:
10591 Renumbered 29831
18/4/51.
29820 (ex60154) 15/8/52.
29802 (ex60156) 19/12/53.
29833 (ex60513) 17/12/55.
29874 (ex60114) 27/4/57.
29841 (ex60159) 26/9/58.
29817 (ex60160) 4/5/60.
29803 (ex60116) 12/11/62.

SHEDS:
Gateshead.
York 20/11/60.
Neville Hill 28/7/63.

CONDEMNED:
4/10/65.
Sold for scrap 11/65 to
T.W.Ward, Beighton.

60155
BORDERER from 3/51.

Doncaster 2049.

To traffic 29/9/49.

REPAIRS:
Don.2–13/1/50.**C/L.**
Don.23–24/3/50.Weigh.
Don.3/4/50.Weigh.
Don.1–5/5/50.**C/L.**

Dar.15/6/50.Weigh.
Don.8/1–1/3/51.**H/I.**
Don.20/4–20/5/52.**G.**
Don.31/8–14/10/53.**G.**
Don.3/1–3/2/55.**G.**
Don.10/5–15/6/56.**G.**
Don.21–27/11/56.**C/L.**
Don.30/7–29/8/57.**C/L.**
Don.28/2–2/4/58.**G.**
Don.21/9–30/10/59.**G.**
Don.12/6–27/7/61.**G.**
Dar.10/9–12/10/63.**C/H.**
Dar.30/1–6/3/64.**C/L.**

BOILERS:
10592 Renumbered 29824
1/3/51.
29874 (New) 20/5/52.
29873 (ex60150) 14/10/63.
29835 (ex60511) 3/2/55.
29858 (ex60156) 15/6/56.
29809 (ex60513) 2/4/58.
29818 (ex60511) 30/10/59.
29870 (ex60515) 27/7/61.
29839 (exSpare) 12/10/63.

SHEDS:
Gateshead.
Heaton 11/9/60.
Tweedmouth 9/9/62.
York 4/11/62.

CONDEMNED:
4/10/65.
Sold for scrap 11/65 to
T.W.Ward, Killamarsh.

60156
GREAT CENTRAL from
7/52.

Doncaster 2050.

To traffic 19/10/49.

REPAIRS:
Don.12–30/12/49.**C/L.**
Don.8–15/5/50.**C/L.**
Don.23/4–31/5/51.**H/I.**
Don.4/6–17/7/52.**G.**
Don.13–29/4/53.**N/C.**
Don.20/10–20/11/53.**G.**
Don.7/12/54–13/1/55.**G.**
Don.16/2–18/3/55.**C/L.**
Don.24/1–3/2/56.**C/L.**
Don.24/4–30/5/56.**G.**
Don.10/7/56.Axle test.
Don.16–23/2/57.**N/C.**
Don.27/5–20/6/57.**C/L.**
Don.19/11–21/12/57.**G.**
Don.2–11/6/58.**N/C.**
Don.26/2–6/3/59.**C/L.**
Don.17/8–23/9/59.**G.**
Don.30/5–14/7/61.**G.**

BOILERS:
10593 Renumbered 29836
31/5/51.
29802 (ex60151) 17/7/52.
29870 (ex60119) 20/11/53.
29858 (ex60528) 13/1/55.

WORKS CODES:– Cow – Cowlairs. Dar – Darlington. Don – Doncaster. Gat – Gateshead. Hay – Haymarket Shed. Inv – Inverurie.

REPAIR CODES:–C/H – Casual Heavy. C/L – Casual Light. G – General. H – Heavy. H/I – Heavy Intermediate. L – Light. L/I – Light Intermediate. N/C – Non–Classified.

60124 still carried Gateshead shed code 52A in August 1960 when turning at Haymarket shed in preparation for its working back to Newcastle. Despite almost ten years redundancy the bracket for the Flaman speed recorder has not been removed.

Another useful view from the tender end shows 60128 at St. Neots on 9th June 1963, working from Doncaster shed. The white flash on the rear of the tender is to warn crews to avoid contact with overhead electrification wires.

60137 working from Newcastle to Grantham, coming off Selby swing bridge when the distinctive North Eastern style signals still existed there.

60133 working from London to Leeds (where it was shedded) in July 1957 is carefully negotiating the down main platform line through Peterborough North station, with *The Queen of Scots Pullman.*

60156 Continued

29802 (ex60154) 30/5/56.
29836 (ex60129) 21/12/57.
29815 (ex60124) 23/9/59.
29840 (ex60506) 14/7/61.

SHEDS:
Kings Cross.
Grantham 9/9/51.
Kings Cross 16/9/56.
Doncaster 5/4/59.
York 26/1/64.

CONDEMNED:
10/5/65.
Sold for scrap 6/65 to
Clayton & Davie,
Dunston.

60157
*GREAT EASTERN from
11/51.*

Doncaster 2051.

To traffic 3/11/49.

REPAIRS:
Don.1–19/12/49.**C/L.**
Don.7–9/5/50.**C/L.**
Don.9–13/10/50.**C/L.**
A.T.C. fitted.
Don.3/10–12/11/51.**H/I.**
Don.7/4/52.*Weigh.*
Don.14–20/5/52.**N/C.**
Don.17–19/6/52.**N/C.**
Don.30/6–24/7/52.**C/L.**
Don.26/1–26/2/53.**G.**
Don.15/7/53.*Weigh.*
Don.9/12/53–15/1/54.**C/H.**
Don.8–12/2/54.**C/L.**
Don.15/11–17/12/54.**G.**

Don.5/4–20/5/56.**G.**
Don.9/7/56.*Axle test.*
Don.22/1–1/2/57.**N/C.**
Don.8/4–9/5/57.**C/L.**
Don.20/10–28/11/58.**G.**
Don.18/3–6/5/60.**G.**
Don.27/11/61–13/1/62.**G.**
Don.26/3–21/4/62.**C/L.**

BOILERS:
10594 *Renumbered 29856
12/11/51.*
29805 (ex60142) 26/2/53.
29825 (ex60147) 17/12/54.
29850 (ex60528) 28/11/58.
29855 (ex60528) 6/5/60.
29802 (ex60160) 13/1/62.

SHEDS:
Kings Cross.
Grantham 9/9/51.
Kings Cross 16/9/56.
Doncaster 5/4/59.

CONDEMNED:
10/1/65.
Sold for scrap 2/65 to
A.Draper, Hull.

60158
ABERDONIAN from 3/51.

Doncaster 2052.

To traffic 17/11/49.

REPAIRS:
Don.12/2–9/3/51.**H/I.**
Don.15/10–7/11/51.**C/L.**
Don.3/10–4/11/52.**G.**
Don.1–29/4/54.**G.**

Don.5/7–11/8/55.**G.**
Don.29/2–5/3/56.**C/L.**
Don.13–18/5/57.**C/L.**
Don.4/10–6/11/57.**G.**
Don.20–30/9/58.**N/C.**
Don.11/4–15/5/59.**G.**
Don.7–11/4/60.**C/L.**
Don.13/8–28/9/60.**G.**
Don.4/5/61.*Weigh.*
Don.27/8–19/10/62.**G.**

BOILERS:
10595 *Renumbered 29828
9/3/51.*
29821 (ex60125) 4/11/52.
29803 (ex60539) 29/4/54.
29806 (ex60114) 11/8/55.
29828 (ex60141) 6/11/57.
29811 (ex60126) 15/5/59.
29877 (ex60137) 28/9/60.
29862 (ex60533) 19/10/62.

SHEDS:
Kings Cross.
Grantham 9/9/51.
Copley Hill 7/6/53.
Grantham 2/5/54.
Kings Cross 16/6/57.
Doncaster 28/9/58.

CONDEMNED:
26/12/64.
Sold for scrap 2/65 to
Hughes,Bolckow, Blyth.

60159
*BONNIE DUNDEE from
7/51.*

Doncaster 2053.

To traffic 24/11/49.

REPAIRS:
Don.6/6–13/7/51.**H/I.**
Don.18/11–19/12/52.**H/I.**
Hay.22/6–9/7/53.**C/L.**
Don.1–26/3/54.**G.**
Don.24/5–6/7/55.**C/L.**
Don.14/11–23/12/55.**G.**
Don.26/4–31/5/57.**G.**
Don.21–31/10/57.**N/C.**
Don.8–22/1/58.**C/L.**
Don.27/10–11/12/58.**G.**
Don.5/4–12/5/60.**G.**
A.W.S. fitted.
Don.11/9–21/10/61.**G.**

BOILERS:
10596 *Renumbered 29844
13/7/51.*
29823 (ex60122) 26/3/54.
29841 (ex60152) 23/12/55.
29867 (ex60506) 31/5/57.
29805 (ex60128) 11/12/58.
29872 (ex60146) 12/5/60.

SHEDS:
Haymarket.
St Margarets 9/9/63.

CONDEMNED:
14/10/63.
Into Inverurie Works for
cut–up 1/64.

60160
AULD REEKIE from 3/51.

Doncaster 2054.

Although 60138 was a York engine, it has here been called upon to work *The Queen of Scots Pullman* **from Darlington to Leeds via Harrogate. It is coming off the 13 chains next to the Midland main line between Wortley and Geldard junctions, to climb up and run into Leeds (Central) station.**

60148 entering Kings Cross station on 25th April 1963 has the 1.32pm arrival from Leeds; Copley Hill had it for around ten years and this was consequently a journey on which it was frequently employed.

To traffic 2/12/49.

REPAIRS:
Don.1/2–1/3/51.**H/I.**
Cow.4–9/6/51.**N/C.**
Cow.12–13/10/51.**N/C.**
Don.22/2–24/3/53.**G.**
Don.20/5–1/7/54.**G.**
Don.4/11–10/12/55.**G.**
Don.1/7–2/8/57.**G.**
Don.28/11/58–9/1/59.**G.**
Don.23/2–6/4/60.**G.**
Don.21/11–30/12/61.**G.**

BOILERS:
10597 *Renumbered 29827
1/3/51.*
29816 (ex60530) 1/7/54.
29787 (ex60153) 2/8/57.
29817 (ex60137) 9/1/59.
29802 (ex60140) 6/4/60.
29859 (ex60120) 30/12/61.

SHEDS:
Haymarket.
Polmadie 14/1/51.
Haymarket 4/3/51.
Polmadie 16/4/51.
Haymarket 22/2/52.
St Margarets 9/9/63.

CONDEMNED:
12/12/63.
Into Darlington Works for
cut–up 9/3/64.

60162
*SAINT JOHNSTOUN from
8/51.*

Doncaster 2056.

To traffic 23/12/49.

REPAIRS:
Cow.28–30/6/51.**N/C.**
Don.19/7–21/8/51.**H/I.**
Don.18/3–24/4/53.**G.**
Don.26/7–27/8/54.**G.**
Don.6–15/12/54.**N/C.**
Cow.22–26/2/55.**N/C.**
Don.10/1–18/2/56.**G.**
Don.9–18/4/56.**C/L.**
Don.21/8–28/9/57.**G.**
Don.18/12/58–29/1/59.**G.**
Don.2/3–14/4/60.**G.**
Don.29/9–16/11/61.**G.**
Don.14/2–10/3/62.**N/C.**
Cow.6–23/8/62.**C/L.**
Don.8–24/7/63.**C/L.**

BOILERS:
10599 *Renumbered 29846
21/8/51.*
29804 (ex60528) 24/4/53.
29803 (ex60158) 18/2/56.
29819 (ex60135) 28/9/57.
29874 (ex60154) 29/1/59.
29844 (ex60122) 14/4/60.
29813 (ex60122) 16/11/61.

SHEDS:
Haymarket.
St Margarets 9/9/63.

CONDEMNED:
28/10/63.
Cut–up Inverurie Works
2/64.

60161
*NORTH BRITISH from
6/51.*

Doncaster 2055.

To traffic 19/12/49.

REPAIRS:
Don.18/5–15/6/51.**H/I.**
Cow.2–7/7/51.**N/C.**
Don.6/10–6/11/52.**G.**
Don.9–28/7/53.**C/L.**
Don.4–17/12/53.**C/L.**
Don.4/8–2/9/54.**G.**
Cow.2–5/5/55.**C/L.**
Cow.22/6/55.**N/C.**
Cow.12–13/8/55.**C/L.**
Cow.14–21/9/55.**C/L.**
Cow.24–25/10/55.**C/L.**
Don.22/11–29/12/55.**G.**
Don.1–12/10/56.**C/L.**
Don.18–22/2/57.**C/L.**
Don.23/4–1/5/57.**C/L.**
Don.29/10–30/11/57.**G.**
Don.8–17/1/59.**N/C.**

Don.1/6–9/7/59.**G.**
Don.15/10–12/11/60.**C/L.**
Don.26/5–6/7/61.**G.**
Don.21/1–1/3/63.**C/L.**

BOILERS:
10598 *Renumbered 29841
15/6/51.*
29807 (ex60149) 6/11/52.
29838 (ex60135) 2/9/54.
29823 (ex60159) 29/12/55.
29804 (ex60122) 30/11/57.
29787 (ex60160) 9/7/59.
29824 (ex60521) 6/7/61.

SHEDS:
Haymarket.
Polmadie 14/1/51.
Haymarket 11/3/51.
Polmadie 16/9/51.
Haymarket 29/6/53.
St Margarets 9/9/63.

CONDEMNED:
14/10/63.
Cut–up Inverurie Works
3/64.

WORKS CODES:– Cow – Cowlairs. Dar – Darlington. Don – Doncaster. Gat – Gateshead. Hay – Haymarket Shed. Inv – Inverurie.
REPAIR CODES:– **C/H** – Casual Heavy. **C/L** – Casual Light. **G** – General. **H** – Heavy. **H/I** – Heavy Intermediate. **L** – Light. **L/I** – Light Intermediate. **N/C** – Non–Classified.

Until 1960 Gateshead shed had 60142 and used it mostly for Newcastle – Edinburgh workings. Here in 1951 wearing British Railways blue livery it is leaving Waverley with the up *Flying Scotsman*.

60151 at Grantham on 14th October 1950. It has just been coupled to the *Flying Scotsman* to work it to Newcastle. The close up view of the tender side shows very clearly how well Darlington works could conceal its rivet heads.

In early 1951 and again for the first half of 1953 No. 60152 was at Polmadie shed to work the up *West Coast Postal* to Crewe. The return working was the 12.50pm from Birmingham to Glasgow which it is hauling over Beattock.

A1s are known to have been entrusted with the Royal train workings on a number of occasions as here on 10th July 1957 when the Queen visited army units at Catterick Camp. This was a repeat honour for 60154 because on 13th September 1952 it had taken her from Bawtry on a return journey to Ballater.

Two A1s working in tandem was indeed a rarity and peculiar to a York shed duty. The 9.15am ex–York and the 8.45 ex–Hull combined at Doncaster where the York A1 took them to Kings Cross. When both loaded heavily they ran separately and to work the Hull train from Doncaster, York shed provided a second A1 which went as pilot on the 9.15 am. Here on a Saturday in 1962 60140 *BALMORAL* will detach to take the Hull train leaving 60150 *WILLBROOK* to continue forward on that from York. Evidently the swing bridges at Naburn and Selby could take the 329 combined tons of two A1s.

60154 leaving Doncaster works at the conclusion of a heavy repair in April 1951, presents a decidedly unusual angle which should help modellers with details of the tender used on this class.

60161 worked from the former Caledonian shed of Polmadie for almost two years in 1951 – 1952, its main duty taking the up *Postal* to Crewe from where it returned with this Birmingham – Glasgow train, seen at Beattock summit. It also worked the 9.25pm sleeper to Euston as far as Carlisle, back on the 3.34am sleeper to Glasgow.

York station in the 1950s was an excellent place to see most of the A1 class, even those shedded and working in Scotland passed through on their way south to Doncaster. Gateshead's 60143 has called, heading either for Grantham with a London train or possibly for Sheffield on one for Bristol.

The driving axleboxes of 60153 – 60157 were fitted with Timken roller bearings which allowed them to achieve high mileages between major repairs. When 60155 went for its first general on 20th April 1952 it had done 237,050 miles, most of it on the heavy overnight sleeping car trains between Newcastle and London. Only eight days previously, near Burnmouth, it has at least ten coaches on an express from Newcastle to Edinburgh.

60159 was always an Edinburgh engine and official transfers never made any reference to its working on the West Coast main line from Polmadie shed in 1951. Probably this was due to the move being a short loan of less than a week, to substitute for 60160 which needed a quick visit to Cowlairs works. Certainly 60159 worked to Crewe on 14th October 1951 and was seen returning next day on the Birmingham – Glasgow express. This early view of it shows decorated buffer faces and the carrying of discs, to indicate class of train being worked. That was the original intention, for those with electric lighting, but the use of discs turned out to be very brief indeed.

York shed did not hesitate to use its Pacifics on the through holiday train from Glasgow to Scarborough and 60138 worked it on the 1960 Glasgow Fair Saturday, when it would be heavily loaded. Scarborough turntable was only 60 feet so could not turn Pacifics which then went back to York light engine and tender first. At Scarborough the crew of 60138 are being given appropriate instructions by a shed foreman.

This view of 60138 was taken at York in September 1965 when only thirteen A1s remained in stock. Note that nameplate and works numberplate have been removed, to thwart light fingered souvenir hunters. It was allocated to York shed for the whole of its sixteen years and was one to retain electric lighting. Although available still for traffic, if required, it too joined the withdrawals, on 4th October 1965.

The *GREAT EASTERN* A1 was not so lucky as the ship of that name. If only a tithe of the money spent on bringing that coal hulk back from the Falkland Islands to Bristol had been devoted to preserving this engine, we should still have been able to see one of Doncaster's most successful designs. Here on 5th March 1965 No. 60157 is being hauled into Draper's scrapyard at Hull. *Sic transit gloria!*

No. 2400 about to make its debut, working its first passenger train, from Newcastle to Edinburgh, on 7th December 1922. To maintain Darlington prestige, the first Raven Pacific was hurried into traffic in full livery but still works grey. Note the square lower corners of the front buffer beam.

LIVERIES

RAVEN A2 CLASS

2400 was put into traffic early in December 1922, fully lined and lettered but in the grey painting used for official photography. On Thursday and Friday, 7th and 8th December, it worked into Edinburgh on the 9.15 ex-Newcastle and returned on the 2.35 p.m. from the Waverley. On the 14th, still in grey, it worked to York towing the 4-6-4 electric loco No. 13, for both to be inspected by the NER Directors. It then returned to Darlington for the North Eastern 'Saxony Green' to be applied, and it was in this NER livery, with 24 inch brass number plates, when it ran trials from Kings Cross to and from Doncaster at the end of June 1923. Most unusually, it went into Doncaster Works, from 5th to 14th July, for a change to LNER green painting, in course of which the brass number plates on the cab were removed and the number then displayed on the tender, in 12inch shaded numerals. This style was retained until the engine was ex-Darlington, from a light repair, on 6th March 1929, when the 12inch numerals were transferred to the cabsides.

2401 was booked out of Darlington Works on 30th December 1922 so that it could be entered into stock as a North Eastern locomotive. In January 1923 it got that company's green painting and lining and on the centre coupled wheel splashers it carried the 12inch circular NER coat of arms. Although the nameplates were fitted during April 1924 the engine kept its North Eastern livery, until 18th October 1924, when it went for its first general repair. Out in January 1925 it was in LNER green with number prominently dislayed on the tender. That was moved to the cab sides in late 1929.

2402, 2403 and 2404 all entered traffic in March 1924 in standard green painting, already fitted with nameplates; 2403 and 2404 had the numbers moved from tender to cab in May and September 1929 respectively but 2402 did not get that change until April 1930.

THOMPSON A1/1 CLASS

The CME thought so highly of his 'Great Northern' rebuild that he accorded it a special livery, never extended to any other engine. At the time 4470 went into traffic on 15th September 1945 Doncaster was still turning out engines in the wartime unlined black with only NE on them. 4470, however, got Royal blue (akin to that which the Great Eastern had used) and with two thin red lines to offset it. The first change took place in March 1946 when the tender had LNER restored. On 9th October 1946 Kings Cross shed changed 4470 to 113, still on the Royal blue which was kept until the first general repair, on 28th March 1947. By then Thompson's brooding influence over Doncaster had departed and when 113 reappeared it was in normal apple green with broad black and narrow white lining. Ex-works in October 1948 this livery was retained but on the tender BRITISH RAILWAYS had superseded LNER. This engine underwent two further colour changes – in January 1950 to British Railways blue (but still with broad black and narrow white lining) and in August 1952 to Brunswick green, with orange and black lining.

THOMPSON A2/1 CLASS

First 'painting' of all four A2/1s was the wartime unlined black, with only NE on the tender. In 1946/7 that was extended to LNER but they were still in unlined black after the end of LNER. From July 1948 it was intended that they should have LNER green passenger livery but only 60508 (September) and 60509 (August) were so treated, and with LNER changed to BRITISH RAILWAYS. The other two had this put on whilst still in unlined black, 60510 in April 1948 and 60507 as late as October 1948.

In May 1949 this class was included in those to have Brunswick green, with orange and black lining and they were so treated from June 1949, with 60509 in June 1950 the last to get it. After that their only change was from the emblem to the crest.

THOMPSON A2/2 CLASS

The quite unnecessary demise of the 2-8-2 engines was appropriately marked by putting their rebuilt form as 4-6-2s into black paint, simply slapped on by wartime labour, completely bereft of lining and carrying only NE on the tender. Improvement however, almost coincided with Thompson's retirement at the end of June 1946. For exhibition in Edinburgh on 19th and 20th June to mark the centenary of the railway reaching there from Berwick, Cowlairs turned out 2001 specially painted in LNER green with usual black and white lining. By the end of the LNER four of the other five had been so treated, leaving only No. 504 in black. That one also got apple green painting, from March 1948 but carrying BRITISH RAILWAYS instead of LNER. Between February 1950 (60501) and March 1951 (60502) all six acquired Brunswick green and until that time 60502 had retained LNER on its tender. From 1957 all duly changed from the emblem to the crest of the coat of arms granted to British Railways.

THOMPSON A2/3 CLASS

That CME regarded this design as one of his standard classes and so they were accorded full LNER lined green livery when new, from May 1946 to September 1947. In due course all except No. 523 had their tender lettering changed from LNER to BRITISH RAILWAYS.

From July 1949 Brunswick green with orange and black lining was their standard painting along with the British Railways lion above wheel emblem on the tender. 60523 ex-works on 13th July 1949 was the first of this class to get the darker shade of green but the initial supply of transfers for the emblem had been exhausted, so it came out with plain tender sides. The emblem was duly applied during a brief works visit in September 1949. Starting in April 1957 all had the emblem changed to the crest at the succeeding heavy repair.

PEPPERCORN A2 CLASS

Although all fifteen first had fully lined LNER green painting, only Nos. 525 (24th December 1947) and 526 (9th January 1948) were completed in time to have LNER on tender, the others all getting BRITISH RAILWAYS. Starting with No. 60527 ex works 13th May 1949 all changed to BR Brunswick green with orange and black lining and with emblem replacing LNER and BR. Ex works 18th May 1957 No. 60529 was the first to change to the crest which all then acquired.

PEPPERCORN A1 CLASS

Nos 60114 to 60126 from Doncaster and 60130 to 60152 from Darlington originally had LNER green painting but carried BRITISH RAILWAYS on the tender. When new in May and June 1949 60127, 60128 and 60129 had the customary broad black and narrow white lining (albeit more generously applied) but on a blue deeper than had been used for the A4 Pacifics. The final ten A1s, Nos 60153 – 60162, new August to December 1949, also had this blue painting and the 36 engines in green changed to it from September 1949 (60138) to June 1951 (60152). This was discarded from August 1951 and, ex-works on the 16th of that month, 60149 was the first A1 to be painted Brunswick green. On shopping after April 1957 all received crests instead of emblems.

The other Pacific built by the North Eastern Railway, No. 2401, was booked into stock on 30th December 1922, though it was not then ready to enter traffic. In January 1923 it went into Gateshead Works to be painted in full North Eastern livery. Painting by Gateshead is confirmed by the absence of a lining panel on the end of the buffer beam, which Darlington normally applied. Note also the cut–away lower corners, which stemmed from 2400 having had an argument with a platform ramp at Newcastle, its length giving extra throw–over on curves. No. 2401 retained its North Eastern painting until October 1924.

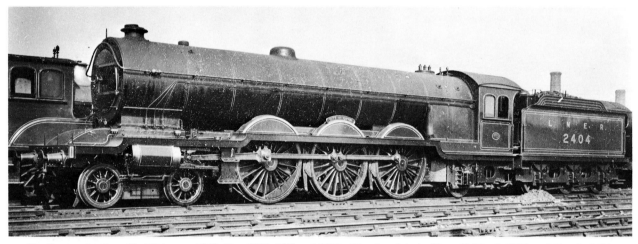

The three ordered on 22nd February 1923, Nos. 2402, 2403 and 2404, did not go into traffic until March 1924, and then had this LNER style painting. When the official photograph was taken in February 1924, No. 2402, in shop grey, had the D suffix attached, but the green paint eliminated it. The three had names from the first, and around the same time the earlier 2400 and 2401 also got *CITY* nameplates. 2401 was to have had a single line name, *CITY OF HULL* but the ex–Hull & Barnsley draughtsman there (who had been moved to Darlington and was Hull–born) emphasised that it needed to be *CITY OF KINGSTON UPON HULL*. A plate needing two lines was duly cast.

2402, on 7th December 1928, and 2404, on 26th September 1929, had numbers moved to the cab, and then had LNER on the tender increased from 7½ins to 12ins. In 2404's case, this coincided with the change to an A1 boiler and firebox.

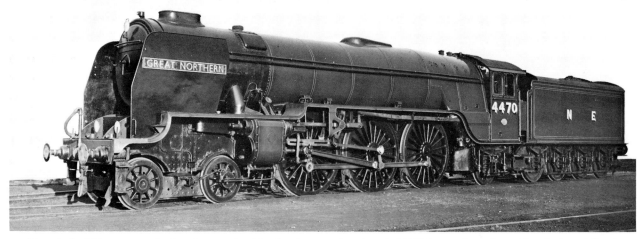

The rebuilt 4470 was not only the sole example of its class but was also the only LNER locomotive to have this painting, of Royal blue with red lining. It was carried from September 1945 until March 1947 when the engine went for its first general repair. After 2 years and 4 months in LNER green, it once again carried blue.

The British Railways blue was a lighter shade than it had previously worn, and the lining was black and white, as carried here at Ganwick, on 8th September 1951. Ex–works in August 1952, it had BR Brunswick green, lined orange and black, which it kept to withdrawal.

Not until after the end of the LNER did the four A2/1 Pacifics lose their wartime black; in 1948 they had been amongst those intended to have LNER green, but only two were so painted. 60508, at Kings Cross shed on 15th May 1949, was one, the other being 60509.

Five of the six A2/2 class had been put into LNER green before Nationalisation, with the last one so painted in March 1948, though with BRITISH RAILWAYS on its tender. This is 60501, similarly turned out by Cowlairs in May 1949.

Unless a tender was *seen* to be in need of a repaint, it was Cowlairs' custom to avoid such expense where it could. 60502 and 60506 thus continued to have LNER combined with BR numbering, the former as late as January 1951.

From July 1957 all six A2/2s changed from emblem to crest, which made them subject to the tenets of heraldry, with the lion facing, correctly, to the left. Four suffered from BR's misguided efforts at having the lion facing front, as with the emblem, and only 60501 and 60502 in the class escaped this indignity. 60504 and 60506 were duly corrected at repairs in 1959 but 60503 and 60505 went to their demise still in disgrace.

The A2/3 class comprised fifteen new engines, all painted in LNER green with broad black and narrow white lining, but No. 519 was the last to have gold blocked transfers. From 520's first appearance at the end of March 1947, the markedly cheaper painted and unshaded characters were used, and the opportunity taken to change to Gill Sans style. Even so, the specification drawing, No. 16601N, was adrift on numerals 6 and 9, which were wrong in having curled over tails. Some of the wrong figures actually survived to the end of steam, on smokebox numberplate castings.

Until July 1949, painting continued to be LNER apple green, to which BRITISH RAILWAYS and BR numbering was applied. 60520 as shown here, got the style when ex-works in August 1948. At that period, Doncaster was making the numerals and letters the same height, but that did not last long.

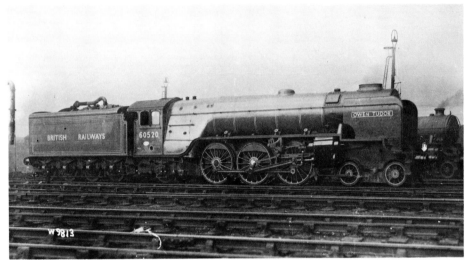

From July 1949 Brunswick green with orange and black lining became the standard for this class, along with the BR emblem of lion over a wheel on the tender. The grant of arms which British Railways had obtained in 1956 brought a change to the crest; the only subsequent alteration, it began to be put into effect from April 1957. Only 60511, 60514 and 60520 escaped carrying the spurious version on the right hand side, but the other twelve were fully corrected.

From May 1949 the A2 class was put into Brunswick green, with orange and black lining, the only later alteration being the change from emblem to crest, effective from April 1957. Nos 60526 and 60532 avoided the defective version, but correction was duly made to the other thirteen.

LNER green painting and lining was the original specification for the Peppercorn A1s but with BRITISH RAILWAYS on the tender. Darlington managed to turn out all its order for 23, 60130 to 60152, in that style. From 60114, Doncaster only got as far as 60126 before there was a change.

From 60149, ex–works in mid–August 1951, all the A1s were changed to this Brunswick green borne by 60130, and the blue disappeared when 60160 went into works on 22nd February 1953. At repaintings, from April 1957, all changed from emblem to crest, and as required, duly bore crests acceptable to the College of Heralds.

The final design of North Eastern tender was this 6–wheeled type, in which the 5½ tons coal space had sloping sides, to facilitate self–trimming. Water capacity was only 4125 gallons, but pick–up apparatus was fitted. New tenders were built in 1922 and 1924 for the five A2 class engines, which retained their original coupling until 1934, when higher capacity tenders replaced them.

After Gateshead shed was allocated ten Gresley Pacifics in September/October 1924, and the older drivers there had accepted that Doncaster *could* build a decent engine, the five A2s were demoted to secondary express duties. By the early 1930s, Pacifics were required to work more intensive duties, but the Raven type was handicapped by a coal capacity of only 5½ tons. In 1934, all five were equipped with this Doncaster 8–wheeled tender, which carried 8 tons and the engines were transferred to York shed to work their heaviest and longest duties.

TENDERS

RAVEN A2 CLASS

From new until 1934, all had 6-wheel 4125 gallons self trimming tenders of North Eastern Railway design. All were changed on the engines returning to traffic, between 13th August 1934 (2402) and 30th January 1935 (2404), to newly-built Doncaster 8-wheeled 5000 gallon high sided non-corridor type, as follows:- 2400 (T5580), 2401 (T5572), 2402 (T5569), 2403 (T5574) and 2404 (T5583).

These 8-wheeled tenders were returned to Doncaster Works in 1936/7, on the engines' withdrawal, to be first coupled with A3 Class 2752 (T5580), 2598 (T5572), 2599 (T5569), 2746 (T5574) and 2503 (T5583).

THOMPSON A1/1 CLASS

4470/60113 had tender No. 5582 from 27th February 1937 and retained it until engine and tender were withdrawn on 19th November 1962. Both were then cut up at Doncaster Works.

THOMPSON A2/1 CLASS

Engines Nos. 3696 to 3699 were ordered originally on 22nd August 1941, as the last four of a batch of 25 V2 2-6-2s and 6-wheel 4200 gallons Group Standard tenders were built for them. On 6th October 1943 Thompson signed a revised order for these four to be 4-6-2 type, but that did not then affect the tenders and they entered traffic with the 6-wheel type. From its first heavy repair on 24th December 1945, No. 3696 left Doncaster Works with tender changed to the 8-wheeled variety. This 5000 gallons example had been rescued from the bombed A4 No. 4469 and had stood spare at Doncaster until restored in 1945 to serve with 3696. It kept its original tender number 5672 until 12th October 1949, when it was altered to 703, in a new series that Thompson started (quite unnecessarily) in 1944.

On 15th December 1945 Doncaster were given an order to build three 5000 gallons tenders, which were numbered 700 to 702 and were intended for use with the other three A2/1 engines, 3697, 3698 and 3699. Instead they were first coupled with A2/3 Class 524 (the final Thompson Pacific) and Peppercorn A2 Class 525 and 526, in that order. Before the three got larger tenders they had been renumbered: 3698 as 509 got tender No. 706 from 26th October 1946, 3697 as 60508 got tender 748 from 15th June 1949 and 3699 as 60510 got tender 749 from 2nd September 1949. All four A2/1 engines and tenders then remained so coupled until withdrawal.

THOMPSON A2/2 CLASS

As 2-8-2s and at their rebuilding to Pacifics, they had 8 wheeled 5000 gallons non-corridor tender. Tender No. 5565 built for engine 2001 was a singleton, because it had a welded tank and

spoked wheels. Tenders 5575 to 5579 put with engines 2002 to 2006 had normal rivetted tank and disc wheels. There was only one subsequent change; in September 1945 Cowlairs swopped the tenders of 2005 and 2006 which then kept 5579 and 5578, through to withdrawal.

THOMPSON A2/3 CLASS

For these new engines, on 12th June 1944 Doncaster were given an order to build fifteen 8 wheeled 5000 gallons non–corridor tenders, and numbers 704 to 718 were allocated to them, 706 breaking the sequence because it was sent to Darlington to be put with A2/1 Class No. 509. The A2/3 original couplings then became 704 and 705, with engines 500 and 511, 707 to 718 with engines 512 to 523 and engine 524 got tender 700. Subsequent changes, all within A2/3 Class, resulted in 60513, 60514, 60515 and 60518 finishing their lives with tender Nos. 710, 708, 713 and 709

PEPPERCORN A2 CLASS

The standard 8-wheel 5000 gallons, non-corridor tender was ordered for these fifteen engines on 4th November 1945. Doncaster allocating the numbers 719 to 733. Instead, engines 525 and 526 came out coupled with tenders 701 and 702 and E527 (as the numbers were transformed to British Railways listing), through to 60538, got 719 to 730. In place of the expected tender No. 731, 60539 had No. 732 (from the next tender order) coupled to it. There was only a single subsequent change, 60530 and 60531 exchanging tenders 722 and 723 whilst in works for general repair during February 1954. The preserved engine *BLUE PETER* still retains its original tender, No. 724.

PEPPERCORN A1 CLASS

In the 700 series of tender numbers, initiated by Thompson in 1944, the tenders built for the 49 engines which became BR 60114 to 60162 were allocated 734 to 782. The first sixteen, built by Doncaster, did not maintain this sequence, 60114 and 60115 coming out with 731 and 733 from a previous order whilst 60126 to 60128 got 745, 746 and 744 due to colour changes in the meantime. The 23 engines 60130 to 60152, built by Darlington, did get tender Nos. 750 to 772 as planned, as did the final ten built by Doncaster, 60153 to 60162, which came out with tenders 773 to 782.

Only minor changes, all within the class, took place thereafter. 60122 and 60126 exchanged tenders 740 and 745 in March 1954 during general repairs, as did 60154 and 60157, which switched 774 and 777 at their May 1960 works visit. When 60119 was withdrawn for sale, to be scrapped, on 31st May 1964, Doncaster shed put its tender, 737, with engine 60158, sending the latter's 778 for sale with 60119.

The fifteen A2/3 locomotives all received new 8–wheel non–corridor tenders, built to the updated version (March 1938) of a drawing deriving from January 1936, for the first streamlined non–corridor tenders. The necessary change from 4ft 3in vertical handrails to match those of 4ft 6in on the cab was missed and the stringent need for economy led to snap–headed instead of countersunk rivets, spoiling the attractive appearance of the apple green livery and lining.

Eight years prior to its rebuilding, 4470 had changed to this high sided, non–corridor tender, which remained coupled to it through to November 1962, when both engine and tender were withdrawn for scrapping.

Nos. 3696 – 3699, ordered in August 1941, were originally to have been further V2 2–6–2s, and through this the customary Group Standard 4200 gallon tender was provided for them. 3696 left Doncaster works from its first heavy repair in December 1945, with this 8–wheel non–corridor tender, which it kept to withdrawal in December 1960. It had been coupled to 4469 when the A4 had been destroyed by bombing at York in April 1942, and had stood spare until rehabilitated for use with 3696. Note that it kept the stainless steel trimming along the base of the tank.

509 had been 3698 until May 1946, and here on Haymarket shed turntable, sometime between 2nd May and 19th August 1946, it still has the Group Standard 6–wheel 4200 gallon tender, originally ordered when the engine was planned as part of the V2 class.

Coincident with the decision to use the spare A4 tender on the A2/1, Doncaster works was given an order for three of the new 8–wheeled 5000 gallons non–corridor type, for coupling with the other three A2/1s. No. 509 duly changed to that type in October 1946, but the other two, had been re–numbered, to 60508 and 60510, before the change was effected, in June and September 1949. This delay arose from the designated tenders being taken for use with new engines of A2/3 class, which Doncaster was then building.

The fifteen Peppercorn A2 Pacifics had identical tenders to those of the Thompson A2/3 class – not surprising really when the latter had placed the order for them in April 1945, intending another fifteen to his A2/3 design. By the time the engines were turned out, Peppercorn had taken over, changing them to his own much improved design. All fifteen tenders had the shorter vertical handrail, and snap–headed rivetting, but the final three, put with engines 60537, 60538 and 60539, had the height of the front plate reduced from 8ft 6¼in to 7ft 10⅜in. The other twelve were so altered at their first repair.

Peppercorn A1 tenders were to the same design as that used for the A2s, from 60537 onwards, and the handrail height remained obstinately at 4ft 3in. Even after 25 years of LNER and then the change to a single British Railways authority, Darlington still showed that it was not *entirely* ruled by Doncaster. The tenders it built for its A1s, from 60130 to 60152, had countersunk rivets, whereas those that Doncaster built, for 60114 to 60129, and for 60153 to 60162, all had the less tidy snap–headed type.

This A2/2 in works grey was photographed on 11th April 1944, on rebuilding from 2–8–2 to 4–6–2. The number 995 is what it would have been given if the Thompson renumbering had not had to be postponed from 1943 until 1946. This engine duly went back to traffic as 2006, *WOLF OF BADENOCH*. There was no change of tender type on this class, those originally built for the A2/1s in 1934 and 1936 (when they were P2 2–8–2s) remaining until withdrawal in 1959–1961.